4 Kids. 4 Fathers.

still winning...

VALENCIA TAYLOR

ISBN: 9798559357690

DISCLAIMER

In this book, you will read about what I experienced in each relationship and other challenges I encountered. The names and locations have been changed to protect involved parties, but my story is true. The people in my story have changed and have grown for the better. There is no hate between myself or anyone described in this book. I have a decent relationship with each individual. This book was not written for those people to be judged because people do change and learn from their mistakes

Table of Contents

Introduction

Being a single mom four times with four different men was never the plan. However, it happened, and if I had the choice to do it all over again, I would. I love my children with everything in me. They are my life. They are my WHY. I couldn't imagine life without them. Sure, I wanted my kids to live in a two-parent home. Who wouldn't? My story just didn't unfold that way, and I had two choices- abort my children or do what I need to do to provide the best life possible for them. I would be lying if I said that I never thought about having an abortion. Yes, I even called and asked about pricing and to schedule an appointment, but the God in me wouldn't allow me to. I thank God that I was raised by a Christian woman, my grandmother. I chose to keep all four of my kids, and they are truly the air that I breathe. In the words of my favorite rapper, "We ain't killing blessings just to please the public."

Chapter One

SENIOR IN HIGH SCHOOL

It was one of those days when we had to wear khaki pants. If you wore uniforms, then you know those khaki pants drew attention. I was standing at the lockers with my girls, turned sideways, then out of nowhere, Jason hit me on my butt. Silly me, I giggled and the rest was history. Jason was chocolate, just what I was attracted to. He was an average height for a highschool teenager, and one of the class clowns. At some point, during that week, we exchanged numbers. It was the end of my junior year. We talked on the phone every day, and he was so nice and sweet. He made sure he found me every morning, every time the bell rang, and basically any time in between. I enjoyed the attention and started to fall for him. When the last day of school approached, I thought we would barely see each other, but he still found ways to see me. I even lied to my dad like I was staying with my friends just to spend time with him. He used to cut hair, so he always had money. He always made sure I ate, and he always made sure I arrived home safely. As the summer went by, we still stayed in touch. I thought I had the perfect boyfriend.

The beginning of our senior year started off perfectly, well at least the first few weeks. Suddenly, I started to barely hear from him, but I didn't think anything of it because he didn't have a cellphone. He always used other people's phones, but he never missed a night without calling me. Everything came to the light one night. This was my first time going to the club and that night I met his "other" girlfriend. She saw us together and confronted him. She was older and had finished school already. I was heartbroken. Later, I started to hear rumors about him and his "other" girlfriend being in a relationship together, and I eventually pulled myself away. Then, I allowed him to "sweet talk" me, and we started dating again.

I transferred to a new school around the end of September because I started to "smell myself" as the older people say and didn't want to follow my daddy's rules. I knew if I moved with my mom, I would be able to do whatever I wanted to do. When I changed schools, Jason and I continued to converse on the phone. Because we were an hour away from each other, there was no way for us to see each other as often as we did in the past. That caused us to pull away from each other. Around January, I moved back to my old school because of my inability to make new friends. My relationship with Jason gained a sense of normalcy again. Well, at least what we thought was normal. We were spending a lot of time together, and I was still lying to my family like I was staying at my friend's house to be with him.

In March of my senior year, one of my classmates looked at me and said, "Valencia you are pregnant!, I immediately said, "No!" She said, "Girl look at your stomach." That night I went home thinking, "She may be right because I haven't had a cycle." After I got past my denial state, I went to my friend's house and took a pregnancy test. Within seconds, the test indicated that I was indeed pregnant. I immediately broke down in tears. All I could think about was that I had ruined my life. My friends and I talked about abortions that day. That night one of my friends told Jason that I was pregnant, and he was happy, surprisingly. The whole time I was thinking why is he happy when I am thinking about having an abortion.

Chapter Two

MY FIRST TIME BEING ABUSED

When I was three months pregnant, Jason and I were at my friend's house where we always stayed to be with each other. I received a phone call from an old high school guy friend who wanted to check on me. I honestly didn't think it was a problem until I felt Jason's hand around my throat choking me. He continued to choke me while pointing to my stomach asking, "Is this mine?" I was scared and confused. Later that night, he apologized and told me that he would never do it again; of course, I believed him.

A couple of weeks later, my ex-boyfriend Keith called. He called to check on me because he heard I was pregnant. Jason was not around me during the call, but I didn't think it was a problem. Later, Jason looked through my phone, he saw the number, and called Keith. Keith answered the phone and Jason became angry. He broke my Kyocera flip phone in half and began choking me, the same thing as before. Again, he apologized and again I believed him. I know- so foolish and naive. The abuse continued all throughout my pregnancy, and each time I forgave him. Silly me. I just wanted to be with the father of my child.

I started college in the fall at MVSU, and he was there too. It had been weeks since our last argument or fight. I was in school, and he was helping me everyday find my classes, and he met me in the union after each class. One day, I saw a classmate from high school who was a guy, and he spoke and we held a small conversation next to Jason. Again, I didn't think it was a problem until I was pushed in the face and accused of flirting with a big belly in the front of me. Honestly, I could not understand why he thought I would flirt with the father of my child standing next to me. From that day, things began to worsen for us. The abuse started again. It progressed from choking to physically hitting me. I hid it from everybody, and I forgave him over and over again.

One day, Jason and I were riding in the car with my step-sister, and he fought me. I was shocked because he had never fought me in the presence of anyone else. I can't remember what the issue was. The fight was so bad that she had to pull over to call my aunt. My aunt met us and she made me get in the car with her. I stopped talking to him for a couple of weeks this time, but I still was in love. I was embarrassed that he fought me in front of someone, which led to my family knowing that I had been abused. I did not want the public to know because I loved him and I wanted to be with the father of my child. Yep, I was very naive. Eventually, I did get back with him, and the abuse did not stop.

Chapter Three

I BECOME A MOTHER
THE THINGS WOMEN GO THROUGH TO TRY TO STAY WITH THE FATHER OF THEIR CHILD

I had my daughter on December 8, 2008. It was one of the happiest days of my life. During my labor, I had so much support. My family and Jason's family were there. My father recorded everything until it was time for me to deliver my baby. When I went in the delivery room, I could choose only one person to go in with me, and I chose my grandmother. I didn't choose Jason because he was young, and my grandmother was a pro at talking people through pain. While I was in the delivery room, there were about twenty people outside the door waiting for my baby's arrival. At 1:14 p.m., Rihanna Mi'Angel Ashantis Allen was born. Everybody screamed for joy, and Jason cried. Jason was very happy. Regardless of our drama, we were the happiest people alive that day. We had our own little family.

When we left the hospital, I went to my aunt's house with my daughter, and Jason came to stay with me. During the first two days, he treated me like a queen. I was convinced that the abuse was over. Around Day 7 after delivery, we visited Jason's sister's house. I was on the computer, thanking all the people who congratulated me on Rihanna's arrival. One of the comments happened to be from one of my exes. Before I could reply, Jason flipped me out the chair, on the floor. I couldn't believe it. I thought we had passed that stage. His sister told him that I had not healed from the pregnancy. He went off on his sister and stormed out the house. I didn't see him for hours; he came back to the house that night, gave me some money and said it was to get Rihanna's Christmas gift. I saved the money and a few days later, he took the money back from me. The abuse continued. It seemed that it would get better, and then it would get worse.

As the winter passed, we still maintained our dysfunctional relationship. At the end of February, the worst of the abuse happened. Jason's sister had a birthday party that we attended together. We had a good night, but Jason woke up the next morning in a bad mood. I was very tired, and he woke up wanting to argue about everything. I told him I was not in the mood. That morning, Jason beat me badly for the first time. He dragged me out of his sister's house by my feet and broke my phone and digital camera. He forced me out of the house with no shoes. It was cold outside, and I had to walk bare feet from his sister's house to his mom's house. Surprisingly, with all the noise and commotion,no one in his sister's house awoke to come to my rescue. That day was literally my breaking point. I left Jason and didn't look back.

A few weeks passed by and Jason's mother was babysitting Rihanna while I was going to school. She called me at school and said Rihanna was really sick. At the time, I didn't have a car. So, Jason's brother came to pick me up, so I could check on Rihanna. When Jason's brother arrived, Jason was in the front seat, and Jason's brother's girlfriend was in the backseat. I hadn't seen Jason since the incident at his sister's house. When I got in the car, Jason said, "Let something happen to my baby. I bet I hurt you". We started arguing, and he jumped in the backseat and started fighting me like I was a man in the street. He hurt me badly, bent my legs back and hit me in my eye that led to a blood clot for days. This time, I thought he was going to kill me. His brother was still driving while all of this was going on. I was trying my best to open the car to get out. I didn't care that the car was in motion. I felt like he was going to kill me anyway. I don't know what stopped him from hitting me, but he stopped, and I just cried. Afterwards, I didn't see or hear from him for a few months.

Chapter Four

FREEDOM, PEACE, THEN JEALOUSY

During the time away from Jason, I was happy and enjoying my daughter. I actually started talking to a nice guy that didn't hit females. Since I was not dealing with Jason, I found a job and purchased my first car. Life was great! Three months passed and I hadn't communicated with Jason. One day, I decided to see if Jason's password was still the same on Facebook. To my surprise, it was! I started reading his messages and learned that he had a girlfriend named Teresa and even worse, she was pregnant! What was I thinking? Why did I go on his page? Finding that out really broke me down. My feelings were hurt. I couldn't believe that he was with someone else and they were expecting a child. Rihanna was only like 6 months at the time. I started stalking Jason's new girlfriend page every day. She was cute, and the more that I looked at her page, it made me want Jason back. I was jealous and hurt.

One day while I was in the computer lab at school, checking my Facebook page, I ran into Jason. I tried to hide my face, but he saw me. He came over and we talked. I don't know how and why, but all my love came back for him after all he had done to me. We started to reach out to each other almost every day. I found out that he wasn't in a relationship with the new girl he had pregnant. He was actually dating one of the instructors at school. Yep, Jason was "getting around." However, he still cared for me and wanted me as much as I wanted him.

A month later, we decided to give our relationship another try. This time it felt different; it felt like he actually loved me and we were going to have a better relationship. We started back spending a lot of time together. Everything was going well. Around October, we were at his cousin's house preparing to go to the fair. Before going to the fair, we got into a big argument. I can recall saying something about him taking too long and I was ready to go. I can admit I do have a very smart mouth, but I never raised my hands at Jason first. This particular time was the worst he had ever abused me. Jason beat me with his fist. Somehow, I got away and attempted to run down the street. Jason caught me by the back of my head and mugged it to the trunk of my car.

When I opened my eyes, I was in a hospital bed with my family surrounding me. My body was so sore. I had bruises all over my arms. After that big fight, we lost contact again. I was done with Jason. I couldn't disappoint my family again. I didn't want anything from Jason, but for him to be a father to his daughter. However, we kept in contact because we didn't have a choice. Jason started talking to another girl named Jasmine. She was a pretty dark skinned girl. I think he was more attracted to her than me because she gave him money and bought him things. The next thing I am about to say, I know everyone that is reading this book is going to call me stupid. Whenever I leave Jason and don't see him for a long period of time or when I find out he has a girlfriend, I always want him back. Yes, I tried to get him back, but this time it wasn't easy. He seemed like he was in love with Jasmine.

As time went by, it was now my daughter's first birthday. Seeing Jason at my daughter's party made me want him back even more. However, I didn't mention anything because he had already proved to me that he wanted Jasmine. It seemed that Jasmine had his "head gone." She had lied to him like she had cancer, but it did not take Jason long to become "hip" to her lies and come running back to me. For some stupid reason, I was happy. I shouldn't have been.

I kept asking myself, "Valencia, why do you keep taking this man back after all the abuse?" And each time I asked myself, I did not have an answer.

Chapter Five

MY FIRST APARTMENT WITH MY LITTLE FAMILY

Jason and I were back working on our relationship. At the beginning of 2010, Teresa gave birth to his second child. I chose to be mature about the situation. I even let him use my car to be by her side for the birth. In the back of my mind, I did not want the baby to be Jason's baby, but after seeing the pictures of the baby, I could not deny it. She looked just like my daughter. Around March, Jason and I decided to get our first apartment together. I was the happiest person on Earth. I had my little family. We weren't having any issues. I was working, and we were going to school. He kept our daughter while I was working, and he also cut hair to earn money to help with bills from time to time though I paid the majority of the bills. That did not bother me because he made sure the house was cleaned and meals were prepared.

Unfortunately, the happiness I felt didn't last long. A full month hadn't passed before things turned for the worst. We were leaving the house one morning for school. Jason said, "Valencia, you always wear that belt tight so your panties can show." My response was, "I have on a belt because the pants are too big." Before I could finish speaking, Jason hit me in my eye. Here I was again with a blood clot in my eye. To make matters worse, he hit me while our daughter was in his arms. I continued to lock the house door, and we walked to the car. I drove to my mom's house because that's who kept our daughter while we were at school. Jason took my daughter in the house and I left him. I didn't go to school that day. I just drove around because I was embarrassed to allow anyone to see my eye.

Later that day, I decided to go home. When I arrived, I looked through the window. Jason was there. I immediately left and went to my mom's house. I knew I could not run forever. I knew I had to face him eventually. Instead of facing him alone, I called the police. They made him leave. He did with no problem, but I knew that was not the end of it. One day while I was sleeping with my daughter, Jason broke in through my bedroom window, knocking my dresser down that had a big mirror. Glass was everywhere. I immediately jumped up and ran to the front door with my daughter. I thank God my neighbor heard everything. As soon as I opened the front door, my neighbor grabbed my daughter, but somehow Jason caught me and dragged me back into the house. I don't know what Jason planned to do to me that day, but God was with me. Before he could succeed, the police burst through the door. Jason tried to jump out of a window, but the police caught him. Jason went to jail and we didn't talk for a month or so, but then, we got back together. I did not understand why I kept finding myself back in this toxic situation, but I did.

I went through so much with Jason, fight after fight. He even had an accident in my car on purpose. We both had just got our school refund check. Jason refused to use any of his money toward bills and other responsibilities because his brother had convinced him that he could double his money by selling drugs. One day, before he dropped me off to complete my work study, I stopped to get something to eat. Jason said he was not hungry, but I knew that was not the truth. That was his way of not wanting to spend his money. I ordered a pizza for just me, and when I returned to the car and started eating, Jason asked, "So, you didn't get me nothing to eat?" I knew he was hungry, but he just wanted me to use my money. I responded, "No, you said you weren't hungry." Jason grabbed my pizza and threw it out the window. Unbelievable, right? After he dropped me off to complete my work study, I started texting him. I told him I wanted to break up and that I couldn't take it anymore. I expressed how I was tired of being abused and mistreated. Why did I do that knowing he had my car? He purposely ran my car into a big trash can behind a gas station. He destroyed the inside of my car. I was distraught. I couldn't believe it. Well, yes I could. Maybe it was that I did not want to believe it. I called the police, but because Jason had left my car abandoned, they could not pursue any charges against him. Of course, Jason called me and told me how sorry he was and that he would pay for my car to get fixed. We broke up again for a few weeks, but of course, I fell victim to his apologies, and we got back together again until one day he drove me on a back road and threatened to kill me. It seemed like things between us would be going good then suddenly, turn bad, and then the worst. That was our normal. Somehow, in my mind. I thought the abuse would eventually stop. I basically was taking the abuse over and over because at that point, I was too embarrassed to let anyone know how big of a fool I really was although everyone knew anyway. I was in denial. One day during the Summer of 2010, I was getting dressed to go to church. Jason came into the bathroom while I was getting dressed and said, "You are always wearing those tight dresses to church." Of course, I replied in a sarcastic tone. Jason hit me while my daughter was next to me. When he hit me, I trampled on my daughter which caused her to fall in our bath tub. That was not enough to make Jason stop. He kept hitting me until my little sister jumped in between us to stop him. Of course, I ended up not going to church. That was the final straw for me. Jason disappeared. We didn't talk again. The next time I heard from him, he had taken a family trip to Chicago and decided to stay. I think that was the best thing for the both of us.I knew God's hand was in that. Either Jason was going to kill me, or I was going to kill him. I think that was God's way of saving me. Our relationship ended in 2010. That was one of the best things that ever happened to me.

Chapter Six

FREEDOM AFTER AN ABUSIVE RELATIONSHIP

Once Jason and I broke up, I remained in the apartment that we shared. After the break up, I felt free. I did not have any worries. The only things I did were spend time with my daughter and worked. It was just my daughter and I, and things were so peaceful. A few months after living by myself, I lost my job and couldn't find another one. I moved back home with my dad. Moving back with my dad wasn't bad at all. I was happy to be around my family again. I actually was back to where I smiled all day every day. For years, I felt like I was trapped in a dark cloud, and finally the sun was shining again. I began to get out more and socialize with people. I was enjoying being single and wasn't looking for or felt that I needed a man.

One day, my ex-boyfriend, Keith, came to town. Keith was kind of like my long distance boyfriend when I was in 9th and 10th grade. Keith was handsome, caramel color, not very tall, he always had all the new Jordans which made him more attractive. Keith and I started back talking on the phone and texting. Keith had a good job, and he only came around on weekends because he lived in a different town. Keith and I started back dating. Keith was nothing like Jason. He did not hit women. He was not perfect, but long as he kept his hands to himself that was a plus for me. We had a good relationship. I attended school during the week, and I also worked. I had finally gotten a job at Wendy's. When the weekends came, Keith and I spent time together if I wasn't working. I was finally happy again.

At the end of 2011, we rented a house from his aunt. Keith still was only able to stay on weekends because he worked overnight. Even though he barely stayed there, Keith still paid the rent every month, and I paid the utilities. Everything was great and I was beyond happy. At the beginning of 2012, we went to a New Year's Party, I drank too much and passed out on the floor in front of the whole club. Keith took me home and helped me shower. I woke up the next morning, and he wasn't home. I wasn't in my right mind that night, so I didn't even know that he left me home alone. I called him, and he said he was at his cousin's house playing the game which I thought was true because he and his cousin played the game a lot.

Keith lied. He was not with his cousin playing the game. I learned a few months later that he cheated on me. I questioned him about it, and he lied for a while. Then, he finally told the truth. He admitted that he cheated with the girl twice, one time being the night that I passed out in the club. I was so hurt, not so much that he cheated, but the fact that he left me at home after I had passed out to go cheat. I couldn't believe him. Until I learned that he cheated, things were great. Our relationship was a definite upgrade from my previous one. After his cheating encounter, things slowly started to go downhill. Keith did everything in his power to make things right. I moved on from the situation and forgave him. Our relationship was back to being perfect in my eyes.

The summer approached, and I wasn't working anymore. I mainly focused on school. It was the summer of 2012, and I was graduating in the Spring of 2013. Keith paid all the bills during this time, and I was so thankful. However, one night while riding with my friends Jasmine and Carlos, Jasmine told me that Keith had been texting a girl named Aysia in an explicit manner. I questioned Keith about it, and of course he lied. So, I reached out to Aysia to see if it was true because I knew her personally. We weren't friends, but we were associates. Aysia told me everything. She even showed me pictures of Keith's penis that he sent her. I couldn't believe it. Why was he constantly cheating on me? If he wanted to be with someone else, why wouldn't he just break up with me? Some men just don't know how to be faithful. Once I talked to Keith and told him that I knew everything. He justified it by saying that that they never had sex. Okay, they never had sex, but that is what he was hoping it led to.

Chapter Seven

REVENGE
CHEATING AND FALLING IN LOVE

When I found out Keith was texting Aysia and saw the facts, my love for him changed. I didn't break up with him, but it was just like we broke up because my feelings for him were not the same. One day, I was venting to my friend Carlos about what was going on with Keith and me. Our conversation was just what I needed at the moment. He made me feel special and gave me so many compliments. Carlos was very handsome, dark skinned, and had the prettiest smile. I never looked at Carlos as anything more than a friend, until one day he texted me and told me he wanted to be more than just friends. When I read the text, I couldn't believe it; I never saw it coming. He said things in a flirting way to me several times, but I never thought anything of it because he was always playful with everyone.

I didn't know what to say. Keith and I were still together. I told Carlos I could only talk to him as a friend. Carlos never gave up and guess what? I finally gave in!

Here I was constantly being faithful to Keith, and he hasn't been faithful to me. Carlos and I started spending time together and going out on dates. We enjoyed each other's company, and we didn't allow things to quickly become intimate between us. We took time to get to know each other. One night, we were at my house watching a movie and out of nowhere, things turned intimate. He made me feel so good. It had been a long time since I had that feeling. I felt amazing. I couldn't believe I had actually cheated and didn't feel bad about it at all.

Once Carlos and I started having a sexual relationship, I completely lost feelings for Keith. I didn't want him to touch me. I hated when he came home on the weekends. I barely called or texted Keith. Carlos had my attention. He made me feel so special and I was happy again. Carlos and I did not want it to be known that we were intimate. He had a girlfriend, but she lived in another state and I had a boyfriend. Eventually, people slowly started finding out because we were spending a lot of time together. However, we were still trying to convince people we were only friends.

My mom's birthday approached, and she had a big party. Keith and Carlos were there. I barely gave Keith any attention because I had honestly fallen out of love with him. Keith and Carlos were staring at me all night. I think Keith could feel that my feelings for him had changed. Once Keith and I arrived home, we did not touch each other. I was just ready for Keith to go home, so I could be with Carlos. I loved being able to be with Carlos during the week. I was enjoying him and was secretly falling in love. One day, things turned for the worse. Carlos ended up going to jail, he called me one morning from jail, and he said, "Sherese I need you." When he said those words to me it's like my heart skipped a beat. I was officially in love with him with no doubts in my mind. My feelings were hurt. I wanted him released. I visited him every other Sunday. I made sure he had everything he needed while he was in jail. I kept in contact with his lawyer, just handling business for him as if he was actually my man. I went above and beyond for Carlos while he was in jail. I did so much to make sure that his stay was comfortable.

During visitation one day, a female named Tanae came to visit him. While Carlos and I were talking she came up to me and said, "I need to talk to Carlos in private. This is about some business." I rolled my eyes and I said, "Whatever you got to tell him you can say it and front of me." She looked at me and responded, "It's whatever. I have bond money right here." I immediately hit her in her face without thinking that I was in visitation at a jail, and most importantly my daughter was next to me. I couldn't believe my actions. I was so mad at myself. What was I thinking? In the midst of doing all that I was a college student with less than a year from graduating. I was also in the field completing my internship as a social worker. We lived in a small town and Tanae's aunt was a social worker.

This was so embarrassing. That was an eye opener for me and I had to realize that I was grown and I wanted something out of life. I couldn't let small things cause me to get out of character.

As time went by, I was still there for Carlos while he was in jail. Keith finally found out about us because one of Carlos' exes, Mya, decided to air our secret. Keith had been hearing rumors about Carlos and me, but I never admitted to it when he asked me about it. We were both cheating and telling lies to each other. Keith came home the night Mya told him everything. The look on his face was like he wanted to kill me. He went into the back room, I grabbed my daughter and my car keys and left the house. Keith had never hit me, and he was not known for fighting women, but the look in eyes was a look that I had never seen. I went to my sister's house and stayed. Keith called me all night and told me to come home, but I wouldn't.

The next morning, he texted me and told me he was gone, and I could go back home if I wanted. When Keith went back to his mother's house, he texted me to tell me that I had until October 1st to get out of that house. It was around the first week of September. He reached out to his grandmother and aunt and told them everything. Keith's grandmother called me. She said since Keith and I were not together anymore, they will no longer allow me to rent the house. I was shocked! When Keith cheated, I forgave him and we moved on, but when I cheated he kicked me out of his aunt's house. I honestly didn't know what I was going to do. I had just started a job at Dollar General Warehouse, working at night. The job paid well, so the money wasn't the problem. The problem was that I stayed in a small town, and it was hard to find houses for rent. I could've moved with a family member, but I was comfortable with having my own space and didn't want to move in with anyone. I continued to pray every day, as the time approached for me to move. I had no luck with finding a new place, and Keith did not make it any better. He kept texting me to remind me that I didn't have much time left before it was time for me to move.

Towards the last week in September, a friend told me about some apartments available in Isola. I immediately called the manager of the apartment, and she told me that it was a spot available. I was so happy and thankful. I turned in everything that I needed the next day. I took her my money order and was able to get the key to my apartment. God is good, he might not come when you want him to, but he is always on time. I was able to move into my new apartment on October 1st. The devil tried, but he did not win!

Chapter Eight

RELIEF AND NO REGRETS

I was enjoying my new apartment with my daughter; it was a lot nicer than the house that I lived in with Keith. It was a three bedroom apartment with two full bathrooms. I loved it! I left the furniture that Keith and I had behind and bought a living room set, a 73in TV for the living room, a kitchen table, and a new bedroom set. When the devil tries to take you down, you have to show him, "What a Mighty God We Serve" and that's exactly what I did.

Throughout everything, Carlos and I were still talking on the phone almost every day, writing letters to each other, and I was still visiting him every other Sunday. We got a chance to tell each other how we really felt about each other. Carlos decided that we were going to be together, and I was okay with us being together. I had fallen in love with him. We never got off the phone without telling each other "I Love You." I was able to talk to Carlos a lot because he had a cellphone while he was in jail, so we talked before I went to school and work. Sometimes he even called when I got off work late at night. By Carlos being in jail, it did not change the way that I felt about him. I continued to be there for him and made sure he had everything he needed.

Carlos ended up being transferred to a different jail in Illinois, so I could no longer visit him. All we could do was talk on the phone and write letters. Even though he was in another state, I still made sure he had food and anything else that he needed. One night, I went to a friend's birthday dinner. Tanae was there. She was the girl I fought with during visitation. There was no bad blood between us because a few weeks after our fight, I cut my foot open at the club, and she helped me. During the dinner party, I went to the restroom and Tanae followed me. She told me I should move on with my life and that Carlos was not going to ever leave his child's mother alone. I honestly didn't believe her because I thought she was jealous. That same night, my friend Jasmine told me the same thing and that Carlos was talking on the phone to Mya and also writing her letters as if he wanted to be with her.

Once again, I was hurt because I was the one who made sure he had everything he needed while he was in jail. I was giving his lawyer money to try to help him get out of jail. I even had gotten his name tattooed on my chest. I was also sending his daughter clothes. I felt played. Carlos really had played me. Everything that he was saying in those letters was a lie. I was so angry. I stopped answering his calls and stopped writing to him. I felt like a fool once again.

During the time that I was down and sad, Keith texted me to check on me. I was shocked and very surprised. He asked to see me. I said to myself, "I might as well because I am single." Keith and I went on a date, and he did not mention what happened between Carlos and I. Keith wanted us to get back together. I told him that we could be friends and see how things go from there. Keith and I started to go on dates very regularly and stayed at each other's house. Things started to get back serious between us. Keith eventually moved out of his apartment and moved in with me. During this time as Keith and I were working on our relationship, I started back answering Carlos' calls when I could. Carlos was still writing to me. Yes, I was hurt that he had lied to me about Mya, but a part of me could not just leave him hanging while he was in jail. I started back being nice to him and writing to him. I was just so confused. I had feelings for Keith, but I wasn't in love with him anymore. Carlos was the man that had my heart. The only problem was that I was scared to give Carlos my all because he would probably get out of jail and break my heart. I continued dealing with Keith because I didn't want to be the one that was played in the end. I began to trust Keith again while in a relationship with him, but I wasn't in love with him.

One day Keith asked me to get the tattoo of Carlos' name covered up. I never thought Keith cared because he had only mentioned me having Carlos' name tattooed on my chest one time. Even though Keith and I were back together, I didn't want to get Carlos' name covered up because I was still in love with Carlos. However, I did it. I felt bad afterwards. The only thing I could think about was what Carlos would say when he found out. Once I got Carlos' name covered up, Keith was happy and started to prove his love for me even more. Keith and I started to work on our relationship and just when things got better, I received a letter from Carlos, stating he had a month left in jail. After receiving the letter a few days later, Carlos called me and told me the exact date he was supposed to get out. When I heard Carlos' voice and heard the words that he was getting out, my heart dropped. Carlos told me he couldn't come back to Mississippi because he would be on probation, so he would have to remain in the state of Illinois. When he said that I knew there was no hope of us actually being in a relationship, but I wanted to be with Carlos, and he made it seem as if he still wanted to be with me. Since I had found out it was almost time for Carlos to get out of jail, I started detaching myself from Keith. I found a way to argue over anything. I was being so mean to Keith and he had no clue of what was going on. With me showing so much anger towards Keith, he eventually moved out of my house. Keith did exactly what I wanted him to do. I just didn't know how to tell him.

A few days after Keith moved out, I received a call from Carlos and he told me he was out of jail. I was so happy and I wanted to see him. I knew Carlos wasn't able to come to visit me in Mississippi, but he told me he would make a way to see me. Carlos and I just continued to talk on the phone and text. Eventually, I started hearing rumors of Carlos moving in with a girl named Courtney. When I heard that he was living with another woman, my feelings were crushed. I wanted to ask Carlos but I didn't feel that I had the right to question him, since we weren't together. As days passed, I started hearing more about him living with Courtney. People were telling me that he only moved with her because he didn't have anywhere else to go, and in order to remain in good standing with his probationary status, he had to have somewhere to stay. Whatever, I am not a fool! I knew it was more to the story than that. Later, I learned that it was somebody that he had dealings with before and they were talking while Carlos was in jail. I did not allow myself to be angry. Of course, my feelings were hurt, but I still felt like it wasn't my place to ask Carlos any questions about it. Carlos and I were living in two different states and he wasn't allowed to leave Illinois, so it was pointless for me to try to make an issue out of the fact that he was living with another woman who was "possibly" his girlfriend.

Chapter Nine

FALLING DEEPLY IN LOVE AGAIN AND GETTING MY HEART BROKEN

While laying around the house relaxing until it was time for me to go to work, I received a call from Carlos. He asked me if I could go get money from his cousin and send it to him. Of course I said yes. I was still in love with Carlos and I would do almost anything for him. I drove to get the money from Carlos' cousin. Once I arrived at the address Carlos had given me, I called Carlos and told him to tell his cousin that I was outside. When I got out of my car, to my surprise Carlos walked up. I couldn't believe it; I had no clue that he was in town. Seeing Carlos' face brought so much joy to me. I was so happy. I didn't expect to see him so fast being that he had only been out of jail for a few weeks. Carlos and I hugged and kissed. At that moment, I was the happiest girl on Earth.

Carlos moved my shirt to the side so he could see my tattoo that was on my chest that used to have his name on it. He tried to look shocked as if he did not know. Carlos already knew that I had gotten his name covered up because

I had written him a letter while he was in jail and told him that I was getting the tattoo covered up. Carlos and I stood outside of my car and talked for a few minutes. We couldn't talk long because I had to go to work. I wanted to call in for work badly, but I had bills to pay, and I couldn't afford to miss money for a man. When it came to earning money and taking care of home, no man could come between that. Carlos told me to call him when I was off work. The entire time I was at work I couldn't stop thinking about Carlos. I watched the time all night; it moved slowly. Finally, it was time for me to clock out. I called Carlos so quickly. When I called Carlos, he told me to come pick him up, and that he wanted to stay a night with me. Of course, I went to pick Carlos up. It had been a full year since I saw him. That night brought back so many memories. I didn't want Carlos to leave the next morning. When Carlos left to return to Illinois, I couldn't stop thinking about him. I was as happy as I could be. Carlos and I started talking and texting more. We both wanted to see each other again, so I made plans to visit him in September.

I drove from Mississippi to Chicago, with my daughter and friend. When I made it to Chicago, Carlos got us a hotel room. I only stayed for three days because I had to get back to school and work. We had a good time while I was there, but the time went by fast and it was time for me to go back home. I fell deeply in love with Carlos all over again and wanted to be able to see him every day. Carlos and I talked about my daughter and I moving there. He told me about all the opportunities there.

Since my lease was about to end and I was struggling in the Master's program, I decided to move to Chicago. I withdrew from school, put my two weeks notice in at my job, and packed. My family didn't want me to leave. They all thought it was a bad idea, but I was in love and didn't listen to anyone, not even my daddy. I let my daughter stay with her grandmother until I was established. I was starting my new journey, I had all types of thoughts going through my head. Was I making the right decision? I thought about my daughter and if Carlos was living with Courtney. As I approached my destination, I got butterflies in my stomach. Carlos told me to call him once I arrived. Once I arrived at the gas station in Chicago, I called Carlos and he met me. We drove to his mom's house. Carlos stayed at his mom's house with me all that day and left that night. Carlos was a hustler, so I didn't question him about his whereabouts. The next day, he came back to his mother's house and we were together again for the whole day and then again, he left at night. I started to wonder what was going on, but I didn't question him. The routine continued: he would come get me, we would go places, he would stay at his mom's house late at night with me and then leave.

Things were moving fast for me. I found a job within the second week. I was determined to get my own place, so I could get my daughter. I did not feel complete without my daughter. That was the first time that I had been away from my daughter for a long period of time. I worked hard the first month, found my own place, but could not move until the first week of November. Carlos and I continued to spend a lot of time together, However, we mainly just spent the majority of all the days and weekends together. One weekend it was his uncle's birthday. That weekend we were supposed to hang out with his uncle. Carlos took me to hotel room, so I could get dressed, and he told me to call him when I was dressed. I called Carlos, but he never showed up until late that night. Carlos came back to the room and went straight to sleep. Carlos' phone rang and "Courtney" appeared on the caller ID. After Courtney called about three times, I answered the phone, but I hung up. I checked Carlos' phone for text messages, but all the text messages were deleted.

Carlos was still snoring, and he didn't have a clue about any of this. I started to wake Carlos to find out what was going on, but then I decided to do it on my own. I left the room and called Carlos' sister, Ashley. I knew she would tell me the truth. Carlos' sister told me that Carlos lived with Courtney, and that Courtney knew about me, but was not bothered as long as Carlos was paying her bills. The news I received wasn't really shocking because I knew it was something going on, but I never knew exactly what it was. I went back to the room and got in the bed, tears started to slowly run down my face, but I quickly washed them away. The next morning, I had an attitude, and Carlos could tell but he had no clue as to why I had an attitude. I never told Carlos about what I learned while he was asleep. Carlos was still tired, so he laid back down. It was a Sunday morning and that Monday, I was going to be moving into my house. Every weekend we'd get a hotel room. Normally on Sundays, we checked out of the hotel, but Carlos acted as if he was so tired and he gave me the money to go pay for the room another night. Carlos slept the majority of the day. Later that day, we went to get something to eat and went by his grandmother's house for a little while, and eventually went back to the room. The next morning, we went to get the keys to my house. When I received the keys, we were both excited. I gave Carlos a set of keys as well. The fact that I had keys to a new place in less than a month after moving to a different state, made me so proud.

Having a new place made it possible for Carlos to spend more time with me. Carlos stayed at least three or four nights out of the week. I assumed the nights that he didn't stay at my house he probably stayed at Courtney's house. For some reason, I didn't care too much or maybe I did care, but I had accepted that, that's just how it was going to be. My only focus once I got my house was getting my daughter. A week after getting my place, I went to Mississippi to get my daughter and all my furniture. It felt great to have my daughter with me. Everything was going well with Carlos and me, with the exception of the known. He never stayed a full week at my house; it was always still the three to four days. I finally questioned Carlos about Courtney. He explained that he had nowhere to go when he was released from jail, and Courtney offered him a place to stay. He claimed that they were just friends with benefits. He said he told her about me and that he was going to be with me. I knew Carlos was not telling the full truth or maybe it all was a lie, but for some reason, I accepted it, I felt like it was the only choice I could make.

At the beginning of December things started to get worse. I found out Courtney was pregnant and of course, it was Carlos' baby. I can't even explain the hurt that I felt. My heart was broken, I never expected that Carlos would get her pregnant. Yes, I knew Carlos and her were intimate, but I guess the naive side of me thought he had enough respect for me to use a condom with her. When I first found out about Courtney that night at the hotel, I should have left Carlos alone. I called Carlos and asked him if he got Courtney pregnant. He paused for a second and claimed that he didn't know if the baby was his or not. Typical man! I knew the baby was his. I wanted to leave Carlos alone, but I moved to a city where I had no family or friends. I had quit my job, withdrew from the Master's program at school just to be with a man. I was too embarrassed to move back home and didn't want to face my family. After finding out that Carlos had a baby on the way, I didn't want to see him or talk to him. I went three days without talking to Carlos, but I eventually started back talking to him. I honestly wanted to kill him, but I didn't want to go to jail. Trust me, If I could have killed him and got away with it, I would have. I still allowed Carlos to come and go as he pleased. How stupid of me?

As time continued, I could no longer stomach the fact that Carlos had a baby on the way. Towards the end of December, I called my friend Felicia to vent to her about everything. She told me that I could move to Texas with her and I could stay with her until I got a job and found my own place. I took it into consideration. Living in Chicago didn't bring much happiness into my life. I made my mind up, I was going to move to Texas without telling Carlos. I did not have enough money to move to Texas right away, so my plan was to wait until I get my income tax check then move. I received my income tax a few days before Valentine's Day, and bought a train ticket to Mississippi. Carlos took Rihanna and I to the train station. He still had no clue that I was planning to move to Texas. I went to Mississippi for a short visit and to take Rihanna to my aunt. It felt great to be around family, people who genuinely loved me. I went out with my friends and enjoyed myself. I needed that. With what was happening with Carlos and Courtney, I needed a revival. I stayed in Mississippi only for a weekend because my friend, Felecia, was flying in from Chicago to help me pack and to drive to Texas. When I arrived back in Chicago, Carlos picked me up from the train station. We both had smiles on our faces and were happy to see each other but little did he know I was planning to disappear.

A few days after arriving back in Chicago, my friend's flight arrived. I picked her up from the airport. Felecia and I went to eat that night and decided that we would pack the next day and leave. While we were packing, I wanted to trash Carlos' shoes and clothes, but the God in me wouldn't allow me too. I called Carlos' mother and told her that I was going to bring his clothes to her house. She didn't question me, but thirty minutes later, Carlos came to my house. I was so shocked and was not expecting to see his face anymore. Carlos wanted to go upstairs so he could talk me into staying, but my mind was made up. He acted as if he was sad, but eventually he started helping me pack. Carlos and his cousin helped us pack everything and put it into the U-haul. Once we were finished, Felecia drove my car and I drove the U-haul- a long nineteen hours to Mesquite, Texas. When I arrived in Texas, I was happy and ready to move forward in life. Although I moved, I still thought about Carlos. I didn't hear from Carlos for like a week. Then I received an apology video from him. From that they forward, we continued to talk and text on the phone and remain friends.

Chapter Ten

SINGLE, BACK TRACKING, & MY SECOND BORN

Once I moved to Texas, I started looking for jobs. I was determined to get a job and find my own place. I moved to Texas toward the end of February of 2014. The first job that I found was at Zales warehouse; the job was easy, but my problem was the traffic. I literally cried one day on my way home from work. I had never experienced anything like that before. I quit working at Zales because I couldn't handle the traffic. I was then hired for Mesquite School District. I enjoyed working at the school, but the pay wasn't much. I knew I had to find something better. I wanted to be able to get an apartment soon. A few weeks after living with Felecia, her mom and boyfriend moved in too. After more people moved in, I knew it was time I tried my best to find a place so I could move out. Finding a place in the Dallas area wasn't as easy as finding a place in Chicago. The rent was a lot higher than Chicago's rent. When I was living in Chicago my rent was $600 for a 2 bedroom house with a basement and a garage. Something similar in Dallas would cost triple. Around the second week in April, I was determined to move and was ready to get my daughter, forever this time. I was tired of the changes, and I know she was as well. I was only six hours away from Mississippi, so I went to Mississippi to visit my daughter every other weekend. Toward the end of April, I was approved for my apartment. I was so happy. I went to Mississippi to get my daughter. We were reunited again, and it felt great.

In the midst of the move from Chicago and the drama with Carlos and Courtney, Keith had eased back in my life. While I was living in Chicago, he reached out to me a few times just to check on me. It wasn't anything serious . Keith and I didn't become intimate again until April of 2014. When I went to Mississippi to visit my daughter, I would stay with Keith. Keith and I were not in a relationship because I wasn't going to attempt to have a long distance relationship. As the months passed, Keith and I got closer. I was enjoying the moments with Keith without any attachments. One day I went to the doctor because I wasn't feeling well. I was feeling dizzy and I thought my blood pressure was up. When I went to the doctor, I was told I was pregnant. I surely didn't want to bring another baby into this situation. I was single and wasn't planning on having another child unless I married. Yes, I was still dealing with Keith, but it was only because Carlos had broken my heart. I needed someone to get my mind off Carlos and Keith filled that position. I never expected to have a baby with Keith. I didn't even know how to tell Keith. We weren't in a relationship, and I am pretty sure he was talking to other females. When I finally built up the courage to tell Keith, he didn't deny our child. He was shocked just like I was, but he sounded like he was happy. I knew Keith would be a good father, but I knew we would never be a family. Everything was cool between us until I learned that Keith was messing around with my step-sister, Kionna. Kionna was considered my step-sister because my dad was married to her mother. I confronted Keith because I considered her family, and although Keith and I weren't in a relationship, I wouldn't have ever thought he would be involved with someone close to me. Kionna and I had a bad "fallen out" because I felt like she was just as low as him for dating Keith. Keith and I stopped talking for a while.

At the beginning of 2015, Keith and I started to have a better relationship, at least that is what it appeared to be. He would call to check on me , a lot more. Around March, I planned to have a baby shower and Keith agreed to help me. Keith paid the first deposit for our decorations and the cake, and he told me he would also pay the remaining balance when that time came. When the time came for us to have the baby shower, Keith did not pay the remaining balance and he didn't come to the baby shower. That was my breaking point with him. I blocked him from my phone that day and enjoyed my baby shower. I couldn't let Keith ruin that day for me. Carlos called and brightened my day. No matter what we went through, whenever he called, he always put a big smile on my face. Carlos and I never lost contact with each other. We didn't talk every day, but he would always call throughout the month. We had a connection that I couldn’t explain and nobody would ever understand.

I was scheduled to be induced May 20th. My aunts came to Texas from Mississippi to be there while I delivered and Felecia was there too. On May 20th at 4:28, I had my second child Jordan J.B Taylor. Seeing Jordan’s face brought so much joy into my life. I texted Keith and told him that I had delivered Jordan. I honestly thought Keith would have been a good father, but he showed me differently. I tried to give Keith a chance to be a better dad, but he left me no choice but to put him on child support. I could’ve handled Jordan's needs and wants on my own, but I didn’t make Jordan by myself, so it wasn’t fair for me to provide for him by myself.

Chapter Eleven

WITHIN A BLINK OF AN EYE BABY NUMBER THREE

Life with my two kids was good. I was happy and single. I was working two jobs- a call center in the daytime and the club at night. I had to do what was needed to take care of my kids. Keith didn't help me at all, but Rihanna's dad did. At first Jason didn't do much, but as Rihanna grew older he started helping out more. My life during that time consisted of me going to work and back home to my kids, and I was perfectly fine with that. Towards the end of the year, I met a guy at a bar named Tyrone. Tyrone was dark skinned, kind of short, very handsome and a gentleman. You could tell he was reared by great parents by the way he carried himself. Tyrone and I talked and texted on the phone for a few months. I really didn't show much interest in him because I was scared to give another man a chance to break my heart. Tyrone offered to take me out several times, but I always made up an excuse to not go. After 4 months of talking to him I decided to go on a date with him. Tyrone was nothing less than the gentleman I knew he would be that night. He opened doors for me and paid for everything.

Months passed and Tyrone and I were still dating. I would let him visit once my kids were asleep. I was not going to allow him to meet my kids, especially my daughter. I did enjoy spending time with Tyrone, but I wasn't going to let him meet my kids unless I felt like we were going to actually be in a relationship for a long time. Everything was cool between us until one day as I was scrolling down my timeline on Facebook and noticed a woman named Evelyn tagged Tyrone in a picture. It was a picture of her laying in a hospital bed and Tyrone was sitting in the room. Her caption read, "He is always by my side." I was so shocked! I looked at her page and she had a lot of pictures of her and Tyrone together, but on his page he didn't have any pictures of her. I immediately texted Tyrone and he didn't text back. I sent him the picture that I saw on facebook, and he still didn't text back. The next day he texted me and told me that it wasn't what I thought. They are friends and he went to see her because she was sick. I didn't know what to believe, so I had no choice but to send Evelyn a message. I wanted to know the truth, and I refused to be played by another man. I sent Evelyn a message, with no disrespect. The message read," Hello, I noticed yesterday you posted a picture of Tyrone. I am not writing to you to start any mess. I just want to know if you and Tyrone are in a relationship. He told me that you all were just friends, but looking at your page, that story doesn't sit right with me. I just want to know the truth, so I can remove myself from the equation. I have been dating Tyrone for a few months." Evelyn immediately responded and told me they lived together, and they had been together for eight years.

When Evelyn told me that, I'll admit that I was so shocked. I can't say I was hurt at all because I wasn't in love with Tyrone. We had been dating for only six months. I just had a hard time understanding how he was able to spend so much time with me. We had stayed nights together, and whenever he came over to my house, he didn't leave until late at night. Once Evelyn told me about her and Tyrone's relationship, I sent him a long message. He apologized and said he and Evelyn were on bad terms. I immediately blocked Tyrone from my cell phone and Facebook and never reached out to him again.

Toward the end of April, I was at my friend Jasmine's house sitting on the couch watching Jordan play with her nephew. Jasmine looked at me closely and told me I looked pregnant. Of course, I denied it. I knew I wasn't pregnant because Tyrone always used a condom, and I hadn't been intimate with anyone else. It had been almost a month since I talked to Tyrone after finding out he had a girlfriend. Two weeks passed, and I noticed that I had not had a cycle, so I went to the store and bought a pregnancy test. I felt like I was wasting my money because it was no way possible that I could be pregnant. When I took the test, I almost fainted. I was pregnant. At the time, Jordan wasn't even one. I laid on my bathroom floor and cried until my eyes were puffy. All I could think about was being pregnant for the third time, by another man, and I was single. I didn't want to call Tyrone. I never wanted to talk to Tyrone again, and definitely not want to have a baby with him. At work the next day, I couldn't work. I kept finding myself in tears. I walked outside to my truck and called Tyrone, but he didn't answer. He texted to say he was at work and would call me back. I sat in my truck and just cried not knowing what to do or say. Within five minutes Tyrone called back. He said, "Hey, Lady!" He seemed happy that I called him. I said, "I was just calling to let you know that I am pregnant and I need you to go half with me on an abortion." He paused and then said, "We used a condom every time. The condom must have broken." I told him I hadn't been intimate with anyone else. He didn't deny the fact that I was pregnant with his baby. He asked, "Are you sure you want to have an abortion?" I said, "Yes", and he agreed to send me the money. I made an appointment at a place called Planned Parenthood. At my appointment, I took another pregnancy test, and they talked about my options. My options were keeping my baby, having an abortion, or giving the baby up for adoption. I was devastated. At that moment I knew I couldn't go through with the abortion. I reached out to Tyrone and told him I decided to keep my baby. He said that he was getting prepared to go overseas to work, so he wouldn't be there physically to help me, but he could help financially. I hung up on Tyrone and blocked him, and left him blocked my entire pregnancy. I honestly hated him, but I couldn't put all of the blame on him. I had to own up to the fact that I was going to be a single mother of three kids.

November 22nd, I went to the doctor for a regular check-up. My due date wasn't until December 10th. When my doctor checked me to see if I dilated, I was five centimeters. I don't understand how I was five centimeters and hadn't experienced any pain. My doctor told me to go home, get my bags, and go to the hospital. My labor was about to be induced. The labor pain was unbearable with this pregnancy. I actually had to get the epidural. It was my first time getting the epidural, and it was the best thing that I could have ever done. Here it was another amazing moment- my son Kingston Amari Taylor was born. He was actually born four weeks early, but he was my biggest baby. He was seven pounds and four ounces. Kingston and I spent Thanksgiving at the hospital. While sitting in the hospital I did not want to call Tyrone, but I had to let him know that his son was born. When I called Tyrone he immediately answered and I told him I had Kingston. He told me that he was overseas and he would be home soon. I really didn't have much to say to Tyrone, so I ended the call within a few minutes. I have to admit. Tyrone was nowhere near a deadbeat. He wasn't there physically, but he made sure he sent money every month, and he always claimed Kingston. Tyrone and I didn't communicate much. He reached out every other week to check on Kingston and to see if I needed anything. Even though I was a single mother of three, I still managed to handle everything- I paid all my bills, provided for my kids, and still held my head high with no worries. After having Kingston, I made sure I took birth control, even though I had no intentions of being intimate for a while. I still had to make sure I was protected.

Chapter Twelve

THINKING I FOUND LOVE AGAIN & ANOTHER HEARTBREAK

Towards the end of my pregnancy with Kingston, a guy named Joseph reached out to me via Facebook. Joseph had been writing to me on Facebook for years. Joseph and I attended the same college, and he was different in the physical sense of men I previously dated. He was tall and light skinned. Toward the end of December, Joseph finally asked if we could exchange numbers. I gave him my number and we started talking on the phone a lot more. Joseph drove 18 wheeler trucks, and he always had deliveries not far from my house. The first time that Joseph and I went on a date,I enjoyed him. He was very funny, and kept a smile on my face the whole time. We started spending more time together because he had a load near my house once or twice a week. I never thought about having a long distance relationship, but I actually liked being able to see him only once or twice a week. By being in a long distance relationship, we never had time to argue.

Everything was going good between Joseph and I until I decided to post him on Facebook as my "Man Crush

Monday." When I made the post, he did not comment until two days later. He claimed he never saw my post until one of his friends told him about it. I knew Joseph was lying, and I felt like he had something to hide. He kept telling me over and over that he never saw the post, and I eventually believed him. After that day, I started hearing rumors about Joseph messing around with other women. He always said it was a lie. I never had proof of anything that I ever heard, so I continued to have a relationship with Joseph even though there was no doubt in my mind that he was talking to other girls and possibly even having sexual intercourse with other girls. I was just waiting on it to come to the light. Joseph was always good to me financially and he treated me with respect, he even bought my kids things.

Around September, Joseph quit his job. When he quit his job, our communication slowed down drastically and we barely saw one another. During this time, Tyrone called to let me know he was back from overseas and asked if I could pick him up. When I picked him up, he asked if he could stay at my house for a few days. I didn't know what was going on, and I didn't even believe that he had just come back from overseas. I think his girlfriend put him out. I didn't tell Tyrone no because I wanted to give him an opportunity to see Kingston. Kingston was almost one and they never had a chance to spend time with each other. Tyrone stayed at my house for four days, and it was four stressful days. I had to get up an hour earlier than normal to take my boys to daycare, drop Tyrone off at work, and then to be at work by 8:00 a.m. After work, it was the same routine. Eventually Tyrone left. I was happy he was able to spend some time with Kingston, but I was happy that he was gone. After that I didn't hear from Tyrone much. He still sent money every two weeks. Even though Tyrone was at my house for a few days I still talked on the phone with Joseph. He had recently found a new job. I never told Joseph that Tyrone stayed at my house because I knew he wouldn't understand and he would have thought it was more than what it was. Since Joseph had gotten a different job, our calls started to get back to normal, and of course we started back seeing each other more. I knew Joseph was up to no good while he wasn't working, but I just never had any proof.

As Joseph and I continued to date, he started telling me he wanted a baby. Joseph was 30 at this time with no kids. Joseph wanted a baby so badly, but I refused to have another baby outside of marriage. This time, I wanted to do it the right way. I guess what I would not give him, somebody else did. One day Joseph texted me and told me that he had a baby on the way. When I read that message my heart dropped. I honestly knew in the back of my mind that Joseph wasn't faithful, but I never had any proof. My feelings were hurt, and my heart was broken once again. I reached out to Carlos. I knew that I could always vent to him no matter what the issue was and he would always make things better. Carlos told me to come visit him so I could get things off my mind. I thought it was a good idea. I booked a flight to Chicago to visit him. I hadn't seen Carlos since February of 2014. When I went to see him, I had no intentions on being intimate with him. I just needed to clear my mind. I enjoyed my time with Carlos, and felt relieved.

When I arrived back in Texas, I finally started back answering Joseph's calls. He had been calling me private for about 4 days. I answered his private call and he continued to tell me how sorry he was. In reality he wasn't sorry, he was just sorry he got caught. I decided to continue to be in a relationship with Joseph, but I didn't trust him at all. Silly right? Things were going as great as possible until Joseph attended the baby shower of his child's mother. I saw pictures that a family member tagged Joseph in on Facebook. Joseph and his child's mother were hugged up, holding hands, and she was even sitting on Joseph's lap. It was obvious that they were more than what Joseph was telling me. I took a screenshot of some of the pictures and sent them to Joseph. He immediately called me and asked how I saw those pictures. Joseph didn't post anything on his Facebook page, but his aunt posted the pictures and tagged him. Joseph claimed he only did that because his mom wanted him to. I knew he was lying so I blocked him for a few days and he called me private over and over, and like always, I eventually unblocked him. Joseph's baby was born in July. He texted and called me the entire time he was at the hospital and sent me pictures when the baby was born. He did everything in his power to make sure I was happy during the time that his child was born.

Chapter Thirteen

FALLING OUT OF LOVE & ANOTHER UNEXPECTED PREGNANCY

Joseph and I were still together; it was now October of 2018. October 10, 2018 my father passed, and it was the worst day of my life. It seemed as if all that week I had bad luck, the same week I received four traffic tickets. I was so stressed out and depressed. I didn't feel like Joseph was really there for me as he should've been, but he did better after the funeral. Everything was going well with our relationship until one day, a week after his birthday, a girl named Keisha sent me a message on Facebook. She started asking me questions about Joseph. She told me that he was trying to be with her and sent me proof that he was texting her. This was my breaking point with Joseph. I accepted the baby, and he still was attempting to cheat. Keisha told me that they never had sex, but they did go out together one time. This time I had proof and he still tried to lie. I sent him the screenshots to show him that I had proof. I didn't want to hear anything that Joseph had to say. I was at my breaking point. I didn't break up with Joseph, but it was honestly over and he had no clue.

Around November, my friend Tawanna introduced me to her friend's brother; his name was Kevin. Kevin was dark skinned, very muscular, and was ten years older than me. It was my first time meeting a guy that much older than me. Kevin had three kids, had full custody of his youngest, and was in the process of buying his first home. Kevin and I started dating in November. He bought me a nice bouquet of roses, spent the night talking, and focused on getting to know each other more. I honestly thought I found the perfect man because he was so much more mature than any man that I ever dated. He was so polite and respectful. Everything was going good with us until a woman commented under his post on Facebook and referred to him as "baby" as if they were in a relationship. I asked him about her, but he said that she was someone that he used to date a long time ago. I honestly believed him. I shouldn't have, but I did. I learned that Kevin was actually dating the woman that I had questioned him about from the comment on his Facebook post. Someone had tagged Kevin in pictures that revealed everything. I called Kevin the next day to let him know I saw everything, but it seemed as if he had me blocked. I sent him a long message on Facebook. He apologized and he said he would call me and explain everything. I didn't want him to explain anything to me. I was completely done with him. I blocked Kevin and never reached out to him again.

It seemed as if I had bad luck with men. Kevin actually did me the same way Tyrone did me. Both of them were secretly dating two women, and I learned about it via social media. I was completely over men at that point. I couldn't take it anymore. Kevin didn't break my heart, because I wasn't in love with him, but my feelings were hurt, and I was very disappointed. In the meantime, I moved on and stopped thinking about Kevin. I was just working and spending time with my kids. Then the unexpected happened. I was pregnant for the fourth time, by a 4th man. This time finding out I was pregnant hurt worse than ever before. I could hardly breathe when the pregnancy test revealed the results. I immediately called my friend Tawanna and told her I was pregnant. She then called Kevin. I didn't want to talk to Kevin. I never thought I would have to talk to him again in life. After Tawanna called Kevin, he called and talked to me as if we were on great terms. I was still upset with him because of his lies.

In the meantime, I was still talking to Joseph. We weren't intimate, but we still continued to talk and text on the phone as if we were still together. I still loved Joseph and was still in love with him, but I just didn't care for him anymore because I was tired of his lies. When I told Joseph that I was pregnant, he acted as if he was so hurt. He wanted me to get an abortion. He even told me if I got an abortion, he would pay for it. Little did he know, things were really over between us after Keisha sent me a message on Facebook. I no longer trusted him and had made up my mind that it could never be us again. I still continued to talk to Joseph just to pass time and to take my mind off of my situation. I didn't talk to Kevin much. He checked in every now and then to see if I was doing okay. I never really had much conversation for him, but I knew I would have to face him and hold a proper conversation eventually.

In June, it was time for me to find out the gender of my baby, and I decided to have a gender reveal. Kevin and some of his family members came to the gender reveal. We found out that we were having a girl. I was so happy. Kevin had already chosen the name Jazell months before I found out I was having a girl. After my gender reveal, Kevin and I became closer as friends. We started back going on dates almost every weekend. I still didn't consider being in a relationship with him because I didn't trust him, but I was pregnant by him, so it was just good to have him around. His energy towards my pregnancy was amazing, but I still could not forget how he manipulated and lied to me. Around mid-September, Kevin started changing. He wasn't calling much, and we were barely seeing each other. A month later, I found out Kevin was dating someone else. My friend Tawanna called and told me one of her friends saw Kevin at the fair with a woman. I wasn't even shocked. I pretty much expected it.

November 10, 2019, Jazell Janae Thomas was born. Surprisingly, Kevin was there during the birth. I had another beautiful baby to join my other three kids. The doctor sent Jazell to a room for a few hours and Kevin went with her, he stayed down the hall looking at Jazell for two hours. Jazell's father and I were not on good terms during the first few days after after delivery. He didn't seem happy, which was confusing because he had gotten her named tattooed on his neck. However, before Jazell turned one month, his attitude changed, and he has been a great father to her since.

Chapter Fourteen

LESSONS, BLESSINGS & MY ADVICE TO YOU

Hopefully this answers the questions you may have or provide clarification to the assumptions. This is my story, my ugly truth. A lot of the things I have done and endured, I am not proud of, but this is my story. This is a part of who I am. Because I have gone through the trenches, I can advise others to take a different route. I truly believe that we go through things so that we can teach others through our experiences. Sometimes, I look back on the relationships I have been in and think, "How stupid of me?," but all of those encounters have shaped me into the beautiful woman I am today. Most people look at me and make assumptions. Yes, I have four kids by four different men and could have been married many times. If I would have stayed with Jason and accepted the abuse, I would probably have a ring by now or maybe if I would have accepted Keith cheating, I would probably be married by now. If I never had the courage to leave Carlos, I would probably be married by now. If I would have let Joseph cheat and not confronted him, I would probably be married by now. NOOOO! I refuse to settle for less and I will not be mishandled. I will not accept abuse or cheating. I will not stay with a man or force a relationship just for the sake of a child. I know my worth and I know what I deserve. When I am in a relationship with a man, I am with him 100%, but I will never tolerate a man's disrespect. I will not sit around and be abused and mistreated, just to possibly get a ring. If I have to accept any and everything from a man to get a ring, then I don't want a ring. Of course, I would love to be married and give my children a two-parent home, but I refuse to settle for less. Will I ever get a ring? I don't know. As long as I have my four beautiful children, I am at peace. I will grow old and be single before I settle for any man that's not making me happy.

My advice to those who may be in a similar situation as mine. Your life is not over because you are a single mom. I see so many single mothers who feel defeated just because the father is absent or just because they are not in a relationship with their child's father. Life goes on. You still have a purpose. Your children are depending on you. Your children are looking up to you. You have not lost. Even as a single mom, YOU CAN STILL WIN.

Dedications

First, I would like to **THANK GOD** for my four beautiful children and for being a forgiving God and never giving up on me.

To my father- May you continue to rest in heaven. Thank you for being a great father, even when I became a grown woman. You still provided for me and gave me everything I asked you for. I love you forever.

To my children- Rihanna, Jordan, Kingston, & Jazell. I love you all more than I can explain. I thank God for bringing you all into my life. All of you give me hope when I feel like giving up. You all are the reason that I never give up. I wouldn't trade any of you for anything in this world.

To my grandmother- Thank you for raising me, I know I didn't always listen. Now that I'm older, I understand all of the lessons you tried to teach me. Thanks for never giving up on me, no matter how disobedient I was. Thank you for never leaving my side.

To my mother- Thanks for always being there for my children. Any time that I need your help with my kids, you drop everything and come to my rescue.

To my aunts & uncles- Thanks for always being another mother & father to me; you all have always been by my side.

To my kids' fathers- Thank you all for giving me the greatest gifts on Earth. Our differences do not change the fact that we shared in creating our greatest blessings.

To my friends- Thanks for being a listening ear, when I needed to vent. Thanks for never judging me and always giving good advice.

To Erica Boyd- Thanks for giving me a chance, giving me hope, and helping me to believe in myself. So many of the statuses you posted on Facebook throughout the years have touched me. Thanks for being patient with me throughout the process of writing my book and never getting upset when I didn't reach a deadline.

About the Author

Valencia Taylor was born in Chicago, Illinois, raised in Mississippi, and currently resides in Texas. She is a single mother of four children; Rihanna, Jordan, Kingston, & Jazell. Valencia received her high school diploma from Humphreys County High School, and she received her Bachelor's Degree in Social Work from Mississippi Valley State University. Valencia is currently focusing on establishing small businesses of her own. She has started a clothing company, "Valencia's Fashion Factory." She is currently working to start her own credit repair company, "JB Quick Financial Services LLC."

Para algunas personas, los dolores de cabeza son tan sólo un pretexto útil para evadir algún compromiso; por ejemplo, salir temprano del trabajo, evitar tener relaciones sexuales. Sin embargo, para muchas otras, las cefaleas (nombre médico que reciben los dolores de cabeza) son una verdadera tortura que les acompaña por varias horas y a veces hasta días, impidiéndoles realizar sus actividades como profesionistas, estudiantes, esposos y padres de familia.

Existen varios tipos de dolores de cabeza; los más comunes son las *cefaleas tensionales,* causadas precisamente por la tensión, ya sea física o emocional; éste es el típico dolor que sentimos cuando estamos bajo estrés, nos sentimos fatigados, tenemos fiebre o cuando nos asoleamos mucho y que, tomando cualquier analgésico, desaparece en menos de una hora.

En este caso se trata de un dolor de leve a mediana intensidad, generalmente en forma de una banda que oprime la cabeza, como si tuviéramos puesto un sombrero muy apretado; otras veces, se presenta un dolor que comienza en la nuca y sube hacia la cabeza.

Estos dolores de cabeza pueden ser precipitados por cualquier estímulo que provoque aumento en la tensión muscular: una corriente de aire frío o una postura defectuosa pueden ser suficientes para desencadenarlo.

Sin embargo, las causas más comunes de tensión son las reacciones emocionales. Los estados depresivos moderados, la ansiedad, el resentimiento, la hostilidad, los enojos, la frustración, entre otros sentimientos, son capaces de producir dolores de cabeza tensionales. En la mayoría de los casos no se acompaña de otros síntomas, aunque en ocasiones se puede presentar con sensación de vértigo.

Por lo general, las cefaleas tensionales no son de cuidado, siempre y cuando no aparezcan con demasiada frecuencia y se puedan controlar rápidamente, ya sea con medicamento o con alguna otra terapia alternativa.

Otro tipo de dolor de cabeza, también muy común, es la *migraña*, que tiene una causa genética; es decir, un factor hereditario. Si padece de migraña, pregunte entre sus familiares, porque en el 80% de los casos habrá algún familiar directo que también la padezca.

La migraña no se cura, pero se puede controlar al grado que tan sólo se presenten uno o dos ataques al año. No se conocen los mecanismos por los cuales se disparan los ataques; sin embargo, se sabe que este dolor es causado por una dilatación de los vasos sanguíneos. Se presenta siempre como un dolor intenso, palpitante, en la mitad derecha o izquierda de la cabeza, pudiendo cambiar de lado en los diferentes ataques. Por lo general se acompaña de otros síntomas como náusea, vómito, aumento de dolor con el ruido (fonofobia), la luz (fotofobia) o el movimiento.

Los ataques pueden durar desde cuatro hasta 72 horas; el 20% de quienes sufren migraña tiene un aviso al que se llama "aura", unos 20 minutos antes del dolor. Este aviso puede presentarse como lucecitas en forma de puntos o rayas, visión borrosa o partes ciegas del campo visual; también puede haber cansancio extremo o irritabilidad antes del ataque de migraña.

En las mujeres, la migraña se presenta tres o cuatro veces más frecuentemente que en los hombres. Esto se debe a que uno de los disparadores de la migraña son los cambios hormonales que sufren las mujeres, sobre todo entre los 25 y los 55 años de edad. Muchas mujeres sufren de **migraña menstrual**, un dolor de cabeza que aparece como consecuencia de los cambios hormonales en este periodo y se presenta antes o durante estos días.

Además de los cambios hormonales, existen otros disparadores de los ataques de migraña, éstos varían de persona a persona, pero los más comunes son ciertos alimentos como el chocolate, los quesos añejos, el alcohol, el glutamato monosódico que se encuentra en la comida china y los embutidos, entre otros. Otros disparadores de la migraña pueden ser la falta o el exceso de sueño, la tensión, la angustia, el calor excesivo, el ejercicio y el ayuno.

Para quienes utilizan el dolor de la migraña como una excusa para no tener relaciones sexuales, les interesará saber que en realidad existe una variación de la migraña que se llama *post-coital headache* o migraña poscoital; afortunadamente es muy raro, pero existe. En este padecimiento, el esfuerzo de la relación sexual, pero sobre todo el orgasmo, es el disparador de una migra-ña muy aguda. Hay que aclarar que, en este caso, el dolor se presenta después de la relación sexual y no antes.

No en todos los dolores de cabeza las mujeres llevan la delantera, pues en el caso del **dolor de cabeza en racimo o *cluster headache*** los principales afectados son los hombres, en una proporción de aproximadamente 100 hombres por cada mujer que lo padece.

El *cluster* es un dolor muy intenso y punzante que tiene que ver con anormalidades en los vasos sanguíneos de la cabeza. Este dolor se ubica detrás de un ojo y no cambia nunca el lado en el que se presenta. Generalmente inicia durante la noche y puede durar de 15 minutos a cuatro horas. Su nombre se debe a que viene en racimos; es decir, una vez que se presenta el primer ataque, vendrán de uno a cinco episodios por día, con una duración de algunos días o varias semanas.

El cluster o dolor de cabeza en racimo es un padecimiento misterioso, aún hoy es un enigma de la medicina. No se sabe qué es lo que lo provoca, no se ha encontrado algún factor genético ni tampoco se sabe exactamente qué es lo que ocurre a nivel fisiológico.

Este tipo de dolor de pronto desaparece, tal y como llegó, y puede regresar en unos meses, años o nunca.

Las cefaleas de más cuidado son los **dolores de cabeza por inflamación o por tracción.** Estos dolores pueden ir acompañados de síntomas como náusea, vómito, falta de coordinación muscular, fiebre, debilidad, convulsiones, cambios de personalidad y letargo.

Los dolores de cabeza por inflamación se deben generalmente a una infección, ya sea viral o bacteriana, y que ataca las membranas que cubren el cerebro, es decir, las meninges; éste es el caso de una meningitis. Otras veces ataca el cerebro, en el caso de la encefalitis. Sin embargo, ambas enfermedades ponen en peligro la vida por lo que es muy importante detectar cuando hay un dolor de cabeza de gran intensidad y con fiebre.

Los dolores por tracción pueden ocurrir después de una caída o un golpe, sobre todo si la persona perdió el conocimiento, y son causados básicamente por tumores, infección, coágulos o hemorragias.

¿Cuándo acudir al médico?

En algún momento de nuestras vidas todos hemos padecido de algún dolor de cabeza de mayor o menor intensidad, o con más o menos frecuencia, pero ¿cómo saber en qué momento debemos tomar estos dolores más en serio y acudir al médico?

Hay que considerar los siguientes puntos:

- Cuando alguien que ha padecido dolores de cabeza, de repente presenta uno que es diferente, ya sea que cambie el tipo, la intensidad, la forma o la duración; es decir, que en esta cefalea haya algo que no es como lo que ha padecido siempre.
- Cuando alguien se expresa de su dolor como: "¡Es el peor dolor de cabeza que he tenido en mi vida!", porque esto nos puede hablar de una hemorragia.
- Cuando comenzamos a tomar tratamiento diario para controlar las cefaleas, así sea un simple Mejoral.
- Si los dolores de cabeza lo inutilizan para cumplir con sus labores diarias.

Es importante identificar qué tipo de dolor de cabeza es el que estamos padeciendo; esto se logra poniendo atención a los síntomas que presentamos durante los ataques, así como a las características de nuestro dolor: intensidad, ubicación, etc., para así poder comentarlo con nuestro médico, quien es el especialista que podrá darnos el diagnóstico adecuado.

Este libro lo dedicaremos únicamente a la migraña, ya que la frecuencia con la que se presenta, lo incapacitante que puede llegar a resultar y el hecho de que no se cura –únicamente se controla–, hace muy importante que, quienes la padecen, sepan identificar sus ataques, controlarlos y, en la medida de lo posible, evitarlos.

Mecanismo de la migraña

La migraña ha tenido un papel importante a lo largo de la historia; allá por el año 4 mil a.C., los sumerios, babilonios y asirios que padecían esta enfermedad, la veían como "el trabajo de espíritus demoniacos en la cabeza" y trataban de desprenderse de los "espíritus diabólicos" con una oración a los dioses o inhalando sustancias con olores desagradables. Cuando ninguno de estos métodos funcionaba, los doctores optaban por hacer un agujero en el cráneo de la víctima, es decir, una trepanación, para permitir que los espíritus demoniacos escaparan.

La migraña ha oscurecido la vida de grandes líderes en la historia como: Julio César, Napoleón Bonaparte y Tomás Jefferson; de pintores como Vincent Van Gogh y Claude Monet; escritores como Miguel de Cervantes Saavedra y Virginia Wolf; el creador del psicoanálisis Sigmund Freud y el filósofo alemán Friedrich Nietzsche.

Si estos personajes de la historia pudieron vivir con migraña y ser exitosos en cada uno de sus campos, también nosotros podemos, con la ventaja de que los avances en la investigación médica nos ayudan no sólo a saber más de esta enfermedad, sino también a conocer todas las alternativas que tenemos para tratarla.

La migraña es un dolor que se caracteriza porque se presenta sólo en un lado de la cabeza. Esta característica le dio su nombre hace casi dos mil años, cuando Galeno, el médico personal del emperador romano Marco Aurelio, la llamó hemicrania (medio cráneo).

Esta enfermedad afecta aproximadamente al 10% de la población en general, aunque en los países industrializados la cifra alcanza hasta un 20%; esto sugiere que las características comunes del mundo industrializado como el estrés, las presiones, el ruido del tráfico y la comida chatarra pueden desencadenar migrañas.

El 30% de quienes la padecen experimenta la migraña acompañada de otros síntomas, como náuseas, vómito, fonofobia (intolerancia al ruido) y fotofobia (intolerancia a la luz).

La frecuencia de los ataques dolorosos es muy variada, desde varios a la semana hasta uno o dos en toda la vida, aunque el migrañoso promedio experimenta de una a tres jaquecas por mes, ya que la migraña es por definición un fenómeno recurrente.

Existen dos tipos de migraña:

Migraña con aura (o común)
Migraña sin aura (o clásica)

Aproximadamente el 20% de quienes padecen migraña presenta **aura**, ésta se caracteriza por la percepción de un resplandor frente a los ojos, rayas, niebla, líneas zigzagueantes o hasta un punto ciego; también se siente hormigueo o entumecimiento en las manos y piernas; puede haber incluso dificultad para hablar.

Estos síntomas se pueden agravar a medida que se acerca el ataque. El aura también se presenta en forma de mareo, pérdida del apetito, cansancio o irritabilidad. Estos síntomas pueden aparecer unos 20 minutos antes de que comience la migraña o incluso una hora. Si el aura dura más de una hora, entonces se habla de una **migraña con aura prolongada**. Esta etapa previa no se da en la migraña común, que aparece de manera repentina cuando los vasos sanguíneos se dilatan y producen un mayor flujo sanguíneo que ocasiona un dolor punzante. Por lo general, los dolores de cabeza que comienzan después de la aparición del aura son más cortos que aquellos que se presentan sin aura.

Algunas migrañas se desarrollan siguiendo un patrón de etapas. La etapa del **pródromo** (malestar que antecede a una enfermedad), durante la cual puede haber antojos, bostezos, irritabilidad y euforia; el **aura**, en la que se pueden presentar distorsiones visuales, entumecimiento o dificultad para hablar; la etapa del **dolor de cabeza**, en la cual se siente el dolor, algunas veces acompañado de náusea, vómito, fonofobia y fotofobia. La etapa de **resolución**, en la que los síntomas comienzan a disminuir; y la etapa de **recuperación**, caracterizada por agotamiento físico. Esto es un ciclo completo de migraña, aunque no en todos los casos se presentan todas las etapas.

Las migrañas se presentan en cualquier edad, pero son más comunes entre los 25 y los 55 años de edad y en un 70% se asocia con antecedentes familiares

Como ya se comentó, es más común entre las mujeres que en los hombres debido a los cambios hormonales que ellas padecen. La fuerte reducción del contenido de hormonas femeninas en la sangre, justo antes del inicio de la menstruación, influye en los vasos sanguíneos del cerebro y puede causar ataques de migraña.

No obstante, algunas mujeres tienen migraña durante el ciclo de menstruación y en la ovulación. La migraña durante el embarazo puede ser molesta, pero no aumenta el riesgo de aborto, muerte o defectos congénitos en el niño.

En aproximadamente el 70% de las mujeres embarazadas, la migraña desaparece debido a que el nivel de hormonas femeninas es alto, aunque puede permanecer sin alterarse durante el embarazo. Entre el tres y el 40% de las mujeres vuelve a padecer migraña una semana después del parto.

El dolor de la migraña sucede cuando hay una fluctuación de los niveles de serotonina, una sustancia química del organismo parecida a las hormonas, que actúa sobre los vasos sanguíneos del cerebro, dilatándolos y causando los síntomas de la migraña. Por lo general, aunque no necesariamente, esta dilatación viene seguida de una contracción de las arterias; esto es lo que se cree que ocasiona los problemas visuales que anteceden al dolor de cabeza.

Existen ciertos disparadores o circunstancias que provocan la fluctuación o desequilibrio en la serotonina, causantes de los ataques. Estos disparadores varían de persona a persona, así como también pueden variar en la misma persona durante diferentes etapas de su vida. Los siguientes son los disparadores más comunes de la migraña:

Estímulos externos

- ✓ Frío.
- ✓ Clima seco.
- ✓ Altas temperaturas.
- ✓ Humedad.
- ✓ Cambios bruscos de temperatura.
- ✓ Incremento o disminución brusca de la presión ambiental (por ejemplo, en un avión).
- ✓ Luz brillante.
- ✓ Altos niveles de ruido.
- ✓ Olores fuertes o desagradables.

Disparadores fisiológicos

Sueño irregular o insuficiente.

- ✓ Cambio en los hábitos de sueño (vacaciones, fin de semana, etcétera).
- ✓ Comidas irregulares.
- ✓ Ayuno.
- ✓ Sobreesfuerzo físico (cargar mucho peso, correr, entrenamiento excesivo, etcétera).
- ✓ Duchas muy calientes.
- ✓ Fumar.
- ✓ Ciertos alimentos. (Consulte Alimentos que pueden ser disparadores de migraña).
- ✓ Numerosos medicamentos.

Disparadores psicológicos

- ✓ Preocupación.
- ✓ Ansiedad.
- ✓ Estrés.
- ✓ Perfeccionismo.
- ✓ Depresión.
- ✓ Shock (choque).

Alimentos que pueden ser disparadores de migraña

Muchos alimentos comunes contienen algunas sustancias químicas, en especial tiraminas y nitrito, que ejercen un efecto sobre el cerebro de las personas que padecen migraña, desencadenando cambios neurales y vasculares que terminan en dolor de cabeza. No se sabe a ciencia cierta cuántos dolores de cabeza son producto de los factores alimentarios; mientras algunos especialistas afirman que entre el 10 y el 20%, otros aseguran que hasta un 75 por ciento.

Aunque hay alimentos que más comúnmente son disparadores de ataques de migraña, en un momento dado cualquier alimento puede desencadenar un dolor, ya que los disparadores pueden variar de persona a persona. Lo que puede afectar a una persona, puede no tener efecto en otra.

Éstos son los más comunes:

- ✓ Cafeína (café, té, bebidas de cola).
- ✓ Chocolate.
- ✓ Queso (en especial el roquefort, cheddar, mozzarela, gruyere, feta, parmesano y gorgonzola).
- ✓ Yogur.
- ✓ Crema agria.
- ✓ Nueces.
- ✓ Mantequilla de maní.

- ✓ Carnes procesadas, curadas y añejadas (salchicha, tocino, salami, mortadela, etcétera).
- ✓ Bebidas alcohólicas (especialmente el vino tinto, la champaña y las bebidas oscuras y espesas).
- ✓ Glutamato monosódico (se encuentra en la comida china).
- ✓ Cítricos (naranja, toronja, limón, lima), la piña y los jugos de todas estas frutas.
- ✓ Otras frutas como el plátano, uvas, pasas, ciruelas, higos y aguacate.
- ✓ Ciertas hortalizas como haba, alubias, frijol blanco, chícharos y cebolla.
- ✓ Algunos panes caseros con levadura.
- ✓ Aspartame.

Es interesante señalar que, en algunas personas, el consumo de alguno de estos alimentos no desencadena el dolor, pero la combinación de ellos sí. Por ejemplo, tomar vino tinto acompañado de queso o de pan con levadura.

Cuando los ataques de migraña son causados por la dieta es mucho más fácil la prevención y control, ya que podemos elegir lo que comemos, pero es mucho más difícil controlar los factores externos como los cambios de temperatura.

Si usted sospecha que ciertos alimentos pueden ser los desencadenantes de su migraña, pruebe sacarlos de su dieta por lo menos durante un mes y observe los resultados; ponga mucha atención a sus alimentos, ya que las reacciones a la comida no son siempre inmediatas, puede tomar desde 15 minutos hasta ocho horas para que se produzca el dolor.

El primer paso para poder tratar la migraña es diagnosticarla e identificar los disparadores que están causando los ataques, cuestión que analizaremos en el próximo apartado.

Diagnóstico médico

Para poder establecer el diagnóstico de migraña, el médico necesita por lo menos cinco episodios dolorosos de cuatro a 72 horas de duración que deben tener las siguientes características: localización unilateral, pulsatil, intensidad moderada a severa y agravamiento del dolor con las actividades físicas, además de alguno de los siguientes síntomas: náusea con o sin vómito, fotofobia o fonofobia.

Adicionalmente, el médico debe realizar exámenes físicos y neurológicos que descarten alguna otra enfermedad.

A fin de dar un diagnóstico acertado, el médico formulará preguntas relacionadas con las características de sus dolores de cabeza, como las siguientes:

- ¿Es la primera vez que usted sufre de dolor de cabeza? ¿Los ha sufrido antes? Si es así: ¿Desde cuándo?

- ¿Cuándo se percató de esos dolores de cabeza? ¿Luego de un golpe en la cabeza? ¿Tras un esfuerzo físico? ¿Después de un cambio de clima? ¿Después de comer ciertos alimentos? ¿En una situación estresante o en una situación emocional?
- ¿Qué forma tienen sus dolores de cabeza: opresivos, pulsátiles, punzantes o penetrantes? ¿El dolor es agudo?
- ¿Dónde ocurren estos dolores de cabeza? ¿En las sienes o en la parte posterior de la cabeza? ¿En la superficie o internamente? ¿En un solo lado de la cabeza o en los dos? ¿Siempre en el mismo lugar o varía?
- ¿Qué tan severo es el dolor: moderado, moderadamente severo, severo o insoportable?
- ¿Los dolores de cabeza duran mucho o son como ataques episódicos?
- ¿Sufre otros síntomas que aparecen junto a los dolores de cabeza, como náuseas, vómito, molestias visuales, trastornos del habla, mareos, parálisis, zumbidos, ojos llorosos?

- ¿Se vuelve usted más sensible a la luz y al ruido durante los dolores de cabeza?
- ¿Duerme mal?
- ¿Tiene alguna otra enfermedad identificada en este momento? ¿Algún problema con los ojos u oídos, inflamación de los senos frontal, maxilar o paranasal? ¿Dolor de muelas, hipertensión arterial o problemas cardiacos?
- ¿Sus familiares padecen o padecieron dolores de cabeza frecuentes? ¿Cuál fue el diagnóstico?
- ¿En qué trabaja? ¿Pasa mucho tiempo frente a la computadora? ¿Tiene que permanecer demasiado tiempo sentado o parado?

Y preguntas más personales como:

- ¿Tiene problemas en su trabajo o en su vida privada? ¿Está usted estresado? ¿Siente temor de fallar?
- ¿Se ha sentido irritable últimamente, agresivo, falto de entusiasmo o de motivación?

Para identificar todas estas variantes y para poder lograr un tratamiento exitoso, resulta muy útil llevar un diario del dolor de la siguiente manera:

Diario del dolor de cabeza

Fecha	Hora de inicio	Hora de término	(1) Severidad del dolor	(2) Factores psíquicos y/o físicos	Tratamiento/ dosis	(4) Alivio del dolor
11 de mayo	3:00 PM	7:00 PM	7	11	Homeopatía	7
1 de junio	11:15 AM	2:30 AM	6	–	Herbolaria	10

Claves del dolor de cabeza

(1) Escala de severidad

1 = Nada
3 = Ligero
5 = Moderado
7 = Moderadamente severo
10 = Severo

(2) Factores psíquicos y/o físicos

1 Problemas emocionales/ familia o amigos
2 Problemas emocionales/ trabajo
3 Trabajo/ problemas
4 Trabajo/ éxito
5 Días de vacaciones
6 Fin de semana
7 Ejercicio agotador
8 Trabajo agotador
9 Altitud elevada
10 Ansiedad, anticipación
11 Crisis seria
12 Periodo de post crisis
13 Nuevo trabajo/puesto de trabajo

14 Nueva táctica
15 Días menstruales
16 Enfermedad física
17 Dormir demasiado
18 Desvelarse
19 Clima
20 Omitir o retrasar una comida
21 Otros_______________

(3) Comida y bebida

A Quesos añejos
B Pescados ahumados o curtidos
C Chocolate
D Vinagre
E Alimentos fermentados
F Productos de levadura recién horneados
G Nueces, cacahuates, etcétera
H Glutamato monosódico (comida china)
I Cáscaras de habas
J Cebolla
K Higos enlatados
L Alimentos cítricos
M Plátanos

N Puerco
O Bebidas con cafeína
P Refrescos de cola
Q Salchichas, jamón, tocino, etcétera
R Hígado
S Vino tinto
T Cerveza
U Alcohol (cualquier bebida alcohólica)
V Otros ____________________

(4) Escala de alivio

1 = Ningún alivio
3 = Alivio ligero
5 = Alivio moderado
7 = Alivio casi completo
10 = Alivio completo

Al llevar un diario del dolor de cabeza, resultará más sencillo para usted y para el médico identificar cuáles son los factores que están desencadenando los ataques migrañosos para así, en la medida de lo posible, evitarlos. Además, con este método logrará encontrar el tratamiento de corto o de largo plazo que logre controlar los dolores de manera más eficaz.

Terapias alternativas

En nuestro país tenemos el privilegio de poder comprar cierto tipo de medicamentos sin la necesidad de una receta médica, tal es el caso del indicado para el alivio del dolor de cabeza. Sin embargo, esto tiene sus riesgos, ya que existen algunos fármacos cuyos efectos son muy peligrosos si se consumen a diario. Otros, al ser consumidos frecuentemente, pueden provocar tolerancia –es decir, que el organismo necesite cada vez más del mismo producto para obtener los mismos resultados– o adicción, que es cuando el cuerpo se acostumbra tanto a una medicina que la falta de ésta puede provocar el síntoma.

El caso de la migraña, al ser un padecimiento de repetición, hace que quien la padece tome cada vez más y más medicamentos que se pueden conseguir sin receta, sin siquiera consultarlo con un médico, con el problema de que crean tolerancias o adicciones y pueden causar efectos secundarios.

Por eso, en el caso de la migraña, las terapias alternativas son una excelente opción, ya que cada una de ellas tiene el objetivo de lograr alivio no sólo en el corto plazo, esto es, al momento del ataque, sino también en el largo plazo.

La medicina alternativa, ya sea la homeopatía, el naturismo, la acupuntura o alguna otra, trata al paciente como un todo y, más allá de aliviar el dolor, buscará qué es lo que lo está provocando e intentará evitarlo.

Todas estas terapias requieren compromiso por parte de quien las lleva a cabo y, en muchos casos, el apoyo de la familia, pero le darán la satisfacción de lograr controlar sus dolores de cabeza sin estar expuesto a efectos secundarios que podrían tener más consecuencias que la migraña en sí.

En este libro presentamos al lector estas terapias alternativas y cómo aplicarlas, con el fin de que la persona trabaje en ellas y encuentre cuál es la que mejores resultados le proporciona.

Homeopatía

La homeopatía se basa en la teoría de que la causa de la enfermedad es similar a su curación. Por ello, el tratamiento consiste en administrar pequeñas cantidades de una sustancia natural muy diluida que, si se tomara en dosis mayores, causaría los mismos síntomas que la enfermedad.

Aunque esta técnica ya se usaba desde tiempos de Hipócrates, fue Samuel Hahnemann quien, a finales del siglo XVIII y principios del XIX, desarrolló los principios de la homeopatía.

La homeopatía se basa en una realidad biológica, ya conocida por Hipócrates, que se conoce como la ley de similitud: "Toda sustancia capaz de provocar síntomas patológicos en un individuo sano es capaz, a dosis infinitesimales, de tratar esos síntomas en un individuo enfermo."

Este conocimiento exacto de la similitud entre el medicamento y la enfermedad justifica el objetivo específico de la homeopatía: individualizar al enfermo y su tratamiento, utilizando las capacidades de reacción de cada persona.

Aplicando estos principios, la homeopatía utiliza sustancias orgánicas, minerales y vegetales para estimular las defensas inmunitarias del organismo. De este modo, el cuerpo puede movilizar sus defensas propias en contra de los agentes patógenos, virus y bacterias, y recuperar su equilibrio, desestabilizado por las agresiones de la vida moderna (estrés, contaminación, etcétera).

Los medicamentos homeopáticos, como cualquier otro medicamento, deben ser prescritos por médicos.

Ventajas del medicamento homeopático

1) Eficacia comprobada a lo largo de millones de tratamientos.
2) Sustancias naturales.
3) Medicamentos carentes de agresividad farmacológica, es decir:
   - ✓ No presentan efectos secundarios.
   - ✓ No presentan contraindicaciones.

4) Aptos para todo tipo de pacientes
   - ✓ Embarazadas

- ✓ Lactantes
- ✓ Niños
- ✓ Ancianos
- ✓ Diabéticos, etcétera.

La homeopatía busca tratar a las personas, no las enfermedades; en lugar de disminuir los síntomas, el médico trata de encontrar la causa de los padecimientos; es por eso que realiza una historia clínica muy detallada para encontrar cualquier causa física o psicológica que pueda estar desencadenando los trastornos, en este caso la migraña, por lo que presentar su diario del dolor de cabeza al médico será de mucha utilidad.

En la actualidad se conocen más de dos mil remedios homeopáticos, en el caso de la migraña los más utilizados son los siguientes:

Belladona

Se emplea para quien padece un dolor intenso punzante o palpitante, con sensibilidad extrema a la luz, el ruido y los olores intensos o desagradables, y con síntomas que se intensifican con el esfuerzo físico. Por lo general, los dolores aparecen por la tarde.

Bryonia

Se emplea para quien padece dolor de cabeza que empeora con el movimiento, incluso con el movimiento de los ojos.

En este caso, el dolor suele aparecer por las mañanas e ir acompañado de náuseas y vómito, así como de estreñimiento.

Nuez vómica

Se utiliza para aquellos cuyos ataques de migraña son provocados por los alimentos o por los excesos en el comer o beber, así como por las desveladas. Por lo general, este tipo de dolor se presenta por la mañana y puede estar acompañada de náuseas y vómito. Empeora con el movimiento.

Pulsatilla

Es muy útil para las mujeres cuyos ataques de migraña son ocasionados por los cambios hormonales. También es buena para quien padece de dolores que se presentan después de las comidas.

En este caso, el dolor puede estar acompañado de náusea y vómito; los movimientos fuertes agravan el malestar, aunque las caminatas suaves pueden ayudar a disminuirlo.

Las personas a quienes se les receta pulsatilla suelen ser hipersensibles y muy emocionales.

Fósforo

Suele recetarse para las personas cuyos ataques de migraña se desencadenan con los cambios atmosféricos, por ayuno o tensión emocional.

El dolor se puede presentar acompañado de náuseas o vómito; el esfuerzo físico y el frío pueden aumentar el malestar.

Sepia

Es útil cuando el dolor de migraña es ocasionado por el ayuno. En algunos casos, el dolor produce hipersensibilidad en el cuero cabelludo.

Puede desencadenarse durante el periodo premenstrual y empeorar al agacharse o al tener relaciones sexuales.

Por lo regular, los pacientes a quienes se le receta sepia suelen ser depresivos.

Es importante recalcar que, aunque los medicamentos homeópatas no suelen tener contraindicaciones ni reacciones secundarias, deben ser recetados por un médico, ya que él será quien le podrá dar un diagnóstico adecuado y recetar el medicamento y dosis acertados.

Autorregulación fisiológica

Esta técnica enseña a la persona a lograr cierto control sobre funciones orgánicas que, por lo general, son automáticas o involuntarias: los latidos del corazón, la temperatura corporal y el flujo sanguíneo hacia pies y manos. Se usa generalmente para controlar el dolor, aliviar ataques de asma, rehabilitar músculos dañados por algún accidente, tratar el insomnio y la migraña.

El objetivo de esta técnica es enseñar a la persona a ser un participante activo de su tratamiento. Esta técnica debe ser enseñada por un médico, psicólogo o un terapeuta preparado.

Para medir las reacciones físicas durante la autorregulación, se emplean diferentes pantallas electrónicas:

- ✓ Electromiógrafo: verifica la tensión muscular y la actividad eléctrica de los músculos.
- ✓ Electroencefalógrafo: registra ondas cerebrales.

- ✓ Pantalla para la temperatura cutánea: detecta cambios que indican variaciones del flujo sanguíneo.

En el caso de la migraña, el paciente debe aprender a desviar parte del flujo sanguíneo de la cabeza hacia las manos, pies u otros sitios del cuerpo. Esto se logra a través de elevar la temperatura de esa parte del cuerpo.

Las pantallas de temperatura, que detectan aun ligeras fluctuaciones de calor en la piel, ayudan al paciente a verificar si está logrando elevar la temperatura de sus manos o pies; sin embargo, una vez aprendida la autorregulación, no necesitará de pantallas para lograr su objetivo.

Ésta es una técnica que requiere mucha práctica: trate de elevar la temperatura de sus manos a través de relajarse y visualizar el color rojo o bien, imaginándose que está en la playa o en un lugar muy caluroso. Practíquelo todos los días cuando no tenga los ataques de migraña; una vez aprendida esta técnica, podrá aplicarla en el momento del dolor con muy buenos resultados.

Autohipnosis

La autohipnosis es una técnica que tiene como propósito desconectar la mente consciente y conectar la inconsciente.

La hipnosis, que generalmente asociamos con un hipnotizador dando algún espectáculo, es básicamente una técnica que realiza uno mismo. Sólo así se puede activar el mecanismo bioneurológico que cierra la puerta del consciente y abre la del inconsciente. El hipnotizador lo único que hace es dirigir a la persona para que active ese mecanismo.

Entrar en estado hipnótico se puede lograr sin la presencia de un terapeuta. La autohipnosis es un estado en el que el consciente está, hasta cierto grado, adormilado y el inconsciente está muy atento y sensible a las necesidades del organismo para restaurar o mantener su salud.

Cuando en estado autohipnótico usted pide que cese el dolor, en este caso el de la migraña, las endorfinas –hormonas que secreta nuestro organismo que son los analgésicos naturales del cuerpo y que no son secretadas conscientemente– comienzan a fluir y a aliviar el dolor.

Cualquier persona puede aprender la autohipnosis practicando unos 20 minutos diarios, sólo se requiere estar en un lugar tranquilo, sin distracciones y cómodo. Para lograr el estado hipnótico usted se servirá de frases similares a las utilizadas por los hipnoterapeutas. Puede memorizarlas para luego repetirlas mentalmente o grabarlas. El tono de voz debe de ser relajado, cadencioso y convincente.

Si va a utilizar una grabación, puede hacer varios ensayos hasta tener la versión definitiva.

Técnica

Comience por relajarse mediante esta técnica de respiración profunda.

1. Ubíquese en un lugar tranquilo. Asegúrese de no ser molestado, desconecte el teléfono y aíslese de cualquier ruido que lo pueda distraer. El lugar debe estar en penumbras.
2. Póngase ropa cómoda, quítese reloj, pulseras, lentes, incluso de contacto; debe sentirse libre y ligero.

3. Siéntese confortablemente, cierre los ojos y comience a tomar conciencia de su respiración.
4. Respire por la nariz de manera natural, lenta y profundamente, desde el diafragma. Notará que su estómago sube y baja.
5. Concéntrese únicamente en respirar. Hágalo unas seis veces y comience con la autohipnosis, tratando de mantener el mismo ritmo de respiración durante todo el ejercicio.

Repita mentalmente las siguientes instrucciones o escúchelas en una cinta preparada por usted.

1. Te estás relajando; estás aflojando los músculos rígidos; están más sueltos. Son como bandas de goma elástica sin estirar. Están flácidos, cuelgan. Todo tu cuerpo se ha aflojado, está flácido. Te sientes relajado... cada vez más relajado... muy relajado.
2. Piensa en tus pies; visualízalos. Todavía están un poco rígidos. Deja que se pongan flácidos... totalmente flácidos. Deja que se pongan pesados... más pesados.
3. Piensa en todo tu cuerpo. Visualízalo. Estás relajado... cada vez más relajado.

4. Piensa en las pantorrillas y los muslos. Visualízalos. Todavía están un poco rígidos. Deja que tus músculos se pongan flácidos… totalmente flácidos. Que se pongan pesados… cada vez más pesados.
5. Piensa en todo tu cuerpo. Visualízalo. Estás relajado… cada vez más relajado.
6. Piensa en los músculos de tu estómago. Visualízalos. Todavía están un poco rígidos. Deja que se pongan flácidos… cada vez más flácidos. Deja que se pongan pesados… los sientes muy pesados.
7. Piensa en todo tu cuerpo. Visualízalo. Está relajado… cada vez más relajado.
8. Piensa en los músculos del pecho y la espalda. Están un poco rígidos. Deja que se pongan flácidos… totalmente flácidos… los sientes pesados… cada vez más pesados.
9. Piensa en todo tu cuerpo. Visualízalo. Está relajado… cada vez más relajado.
10. Piensa en los músculos de tus brazos. Se sienten rígidos. Deja que se pongan flácidos… cada

vez más flácidos. Los sientes pesados... cada vez más pesados.

11. Piensa en todo tu cuerpo. Visualízalo. Está relajado... cada vez más relajado. Piensa en tus pies... se sienten muy relajados. Piensa en tus pantorrillas y en tus muslos. Están totalmente relajados. Piensa en los músculos de tu estómago. Visualízalos. Están muy relajados. Piensa en los músculos de tu pecho y espalda. Visualízalos... están totalmente relajados. Piensa en los músculos de tus brazos. Visualízalos. Están muy relajados. Visualiza todo tu cuerpo. Está relajado.

En este momento del ejercicio, usted está en estado hipnótico y altamente sensible a la sugestión. Es en este momento que le dará instrucciones a su dolor. Después, seguirá con la sugestión poshipnótica.

12. Tu dolor se hace débil. Cada vez más débil... ya no es más que un hormigueo agradable.

13. De ahora en adelante, tu dolor se convertirá en un agradable hormigueo cada vez que cuentes 1... 2... 3... 4... 5... 6... 7... 8... 9... 10.
14. Al contar hacia atrás del 3 al 1, despertarás relajado y con una sensación de bienestar. Abre lentamente los ojos. Incorpórate poco a poco. Flexiona los músculos.

Cuando desaparezca el efecto hipnótico y sienta de nuevo el dolor, ponga a prueba la sugestión hipnótica contando 1... 2... 3... 4... 5... 6... 7... 8... 9... 10.

Si le preocupa no poder enfrentar una situación de emergencia cuando se encuentre en estado hipnótico, añada la siguiente sugestión: "En un estado de emergencia, despertaré totalmente alerta."

Para dominar esta técnica requerirá de mucha paciencia y dedicación; busque la ayuda de un hipnoterapeuta o psicoterapeuta que le ayude a aprender correctamente la técnica, no se dé por vencido si no logra la autohipnosis en los primeros intentos, aproximadamente le tomará un mes de práctica lograr el objetivo. Recuerde que en ésta, como en todas las terapias alternativas, la mejoría está en sus manos.

Aromaterapia

La aromaterapia es una técnica que hace uso de los aceites esenciales de gran número de plantas aromáticas, arbustos y árboles con fines médicos, psicológicos o simplemente cosméticos.

El aceite se extrae de hojas, flores, raíces, semillas, frutos, corteza o resina para después diluirse en agua o en algún aceite sin perfume. Estas soluciones se pueden aplicar como masaje sobre la piel, inhalar en forma de vapor, agregarse al agua de baño o usarse en compresas.

La aromaterapia deriva de la medicina herbolaria, pero usa un solo componente de la planta: el aceite esencial. Los aceites esenciales han sido utilizados desde las civilizaciones antiguas. Se sabe que los griegos, los romanos, los chinos, los egipcios, los árabes, los persas y los pueblos aborígenes de Australia, la India y África han usado aceites esenciales como perfumes, medicinas, inciensos y muchas otras formas por cientos de años.

Los aceites esenciales en la aromaterapia actúan en dos niveles: el psicológico y el físico. En el aspecto psicológico, algunos aceites aromáticos pueden lograr un efecto poderoso en la mente, alterando el estado de ánimo de las personas que los inhalan. Imagine algunos de sus aromas favoritos, ¿le traen recuerdos agradables? Puede ser el aroma del campo, de la tierra húmeda, de algún platillo que preparaba su madre, en fin. El olfato en un sentido primitivo y poderoso que lo mismo nos puede alertar de algún peligro, como cuando percibimos una fuga de gas, que traernos recuerdos o hacernos sentir atracción hacia determinada persona.

En el caso de la aromaterapia, existen aceites esenciales que pueden lograr cambiar nuestro estado de ánimo, relajarnos, estimularnos o ayudarnos a la meditación.

Los olores de los aceites son recibidos dentro de la cavidad nasal por las células receptoras que están conectadas al sistema límbico en el cerebro –la parte del cerebro que controla la emoción y la memoria–. Los olores estimulan al cerebro para liberar ciertos neuroquímicos en el torrente sanguíneo.

Las endorfinas son otro grupo de químicos que también pueden ser producidos como respuesta a los aceites esenciales. Éstas hacen que nos sintamos bien, pues combaten el dolor.

En el nivel físico, cada aceite esencial, según su compuesto químico, tendrá sus efectos específicos en el organismo; pueden ser: antisépticos, antivirales, antiinflamatorios, analgésicos, antidepresivos o expectorantes.

Actualmente existen alrededor de 200 esencias destiladas que son utilizadas para efectos terapéuticos, psicológicos o fisiológicos.

Aunque en su mayoría todas las esencias funcionan para aliviar el dolor, en el caso de la migraña es importante determinar cuáles son los factores detonantes de los episodios para poder tratar directamente ese padecimiento. Esta terapia es particularmente útil para las personas cuya migraña es desencadenada por estrés, ansiedad, depresión o falta de sueño.

Cuando utilice los aceites, tenga en cuenta las siguientes recomendaciones:

Los aceites esenciales nunca deben aplicarse puros en la piel. Las excepciones de esta regla son la lavanda y el árbol de té. Mézclelos con un agente o sustancia base antes de aplicarlos como masaje o mézclelos en una tina. Cualquier esencia vegetal puede funcionar como agente, por ejemplo: aceite de almendras dulces, aceite de aguacate, aceite de coco, aceite de oliva, aceite de girasol o aceite de germen de trigo.

✓ Utilice la siguiente guía para las diluciones:
  - Para una dilución del 1%: tres gotas de aceite esencial por cada cucharada de aceite base.
  - Para una dilución del 2 %: seis gotas de aceite esencial por cada cucharada de aceite base.
  - Para una dilución del 3%: nueve gotas de aceite esencial por cada cucharada de aceite base.

✓ Si los aceites se van a utilizar en inhalaciones, utilice un pebetero para mezclarlos con agua, nunca con aceite ya que son muy inflamables.

✓ Para la inhalación por vapor, llene un recipiente con dos litros de agua muy caliente y agregue unas gotas del aceite.

✓ Cerciórese de mantener los aceites fuera del alcance de los niños, ya que ingeridos pueden ser tóxicos.

- ✓ Busque el consejo de un terapeuta para utilizar los aceites en niños o durante el embarazo.

Para tratar la migraña, los aceites más útiles son los siguientes:

Lavanda/*Lavandula vera*

Pertenece a la familia de las Lamiaceae. Originalmente viene del Mediterráneo pero actualmente crece por todo el mundo. El aceite esencial se obtiene de las flores por destilación al vapor. El aceite es transparente o ligeramente amarillo y tiene un aroma floral dulce. Su uso es sumamente seguro. La lavanda actúa sobre las emociones con un efecto sedante y relajante. Es particularmente benéfica para quienes se encuentran decaídos o se sienten vulnerables o ansiosos. Es excelente para el tratamiento del insomnio. Además, sus propiedades analgésicas hacen que sea conveniente para los dolores de cabeza.

Se puede utilizar en vaporizaciones, inhalaciones, masajes o, simplemente, ponga unas gotitas de lavanda en su almohada para ayudarle a conciliar el sueño.

Rosa/*Rosa centifolia-Rosa damascena*

Hay dos variedades principales de rosas que se utilizan para la producción de aceites esenciales: la rosa de Castilla y la rosa de Damasco. En la antigüedad, el uso medicinal de las rosas en Oriente fue muy extenso para una gran variedad de enfermedades, entre las que se incluyen fiebre, problemas de la piel, digestivos y circulatorios. También se le valoró por sus propiedades afrodisiacas.

Se usa la destilación al vapor de los pétalos de rosa para producir el aceite esencial. Los aceites tanto de rosa de Castilla como de la rosa de Damasco son amarillos, su aroma es dulce, floral, fuerte y penetrante.

El aceite de rosa relaja y fortalece, da una sensación de calma y bienestar. Alivia el estrés y levanta el ánimo. Se puede utilizar en masajes, añadido al baño de tina y en vaporizaciones. Es un aceite seguro, no es tóxico, no irrita, pero no es recomendable durante los primeros meses de embarazo.

Menta/*Mentha piperita*

Hay muchas variedades de menta; la menta y la hierbabuena son las dos que se utilizan para la aromaterapia. Es una hierba que se cultiva en todo el mundo. Tiene una larga historia de uso en la medicina herbolaria. Existen evidencias de que los antiguos egipcios usaban esta hierba para el tratamiento de diversas enfermedades como indigestión, cólico, flatulencia, náusea, dolor de garganta y dolor de cabeza.

El aceite esencial se produce por el proceso de destilación al vapor. Es amarillo verdoso claro y tiene un aroma fuerte y fresco.

El aceite de menta tiene propiedades desinflamatorias y analgésicas, por lo que resulta útil para aliviar el dolor de cabeza. Además refresca la mente y el cuerpo, le ayuda a levantar el ánimo, darse valor y enfocar y despejar los pensamientos desordenados.

Se puede utilizar en baño de tina, masajes, vaporizaciones e inhalaciones. No es tóxico; sin embargo, puede resultar irritante en algunas pieles sensibles. Utilícelo en una dilución de 1% para masaje. Para el baño, tres gotas son más que suficientes.

Salvia esclarea/*Salvia sclarea*

La salvia esclarea pertenece a la familia de las Lamiaceae. Originalmente viene de Siria, pero se ha cultivado en

Inglaterra desde el siglo XVI. Actualmente se cultiva comercialmente en España y Francia.

Se ha utilizado medicinalmente desde la Edad Media para muchas enfermedades, en especial afecciones de los ojos. Es más segura para el uso terapéutico que la salvia de jardín, que tiene un alto nivel de toxicidad.

Tanto las hojas como las flores se usan para obtener el aceite esencial, el cual se extrae por destilación al vapor. Éste tiene un aroma característico a hierba, ligero, bastante dulce y suavemente amargo. Tiene un color amarillo claro. Se caracteriza por su efecto sedante, calma la tensión, sube el ánimo, crea una sensación de bienestar y da un sentimiento de optimismo.

Se recomienda que se use en vaporizadores o difusores, también se puede emplear en masajes. Hay que tener precaución con este aceite, pues en grandes cantidades puede causar somnolencia. Se debe evitar si se consume alcohol, ya que la combinación de los dos puede producir un fuerte efecto narcótico. No se debe usar durante el embarazo.

Manzanilla/*Matricaria chamomilla*/ *Anthemis nobilis*

Manzanilla romana y manzanilla alemana son las dos variedades que se utilizan en la aromaterapia. La manzanilla romana crece todo el año, mientras que la alemana es una hierba anual que crece silvestre en Alemania y Gran Bretaña, entre otros lugares.

La manzanilla ha sido muy apreciada en la medicina herbolaria durante muchos siglos. El aceite de manzanilla es azul y en aromaterapia tiene efectos sedantes y relajantes; usada en el baño puede aliviar el estrés y la ansiedad. Además, tiene propiedades analgésicas por lo que es muy útil para aliviar la migraña. Se puede utilizar en compresas, inhalación, masajes, vaporizadores y difusores.

El uso de la manzanilla es seguro, ya que no es tóxica, aunque puede causar irritación en pieles sensibles. Se debe evitar su uso durante los tres primeros meses de embarazo.

Mandarina/*Citrus nobilis*/*Citrus reticulata*

La mandarina pertenece a la familia de las Rutaceae. El árbol es originario de China, pero ha crecido en Europa y en América por casi 200 años.

El aceite esencial de mandarina se obtiene por prensado mecánico. Tiene un color naranja y un aroma cítrico dulce. Terapéuticamente, el aceite de mandarina es calmante, relaja la tensión y la irritabilidad nerviosa.

Puede usarse en baños, compresas, inhalación, masajes, vaporizaciones y difusores. Es uno de los aceites más seguros y por ello es adecuado para usarlo en niños. Únicamente evite exponerse al Sol en las horas inmediatas a su aplicación en la piel.

Romero/*Rosemarinus officinalis*

El romero originalmente viene del área del Mediterráneo, pero ahora crece en todo el mundo. Pertenece a la familia de las Lamiaceae. Es una hierba que crece relativamente fácil y es popular como condimento en la cocina de muchos países. Durante años, el romero se ha utilizado en la medicina herbolaria; en varias culturas se creía que daba protección contra los espíritus malignos.

El aceite esencial se extrae de toda la planta por destilación al vapor. Es amarillo claro o incoloro. Su fragancia es fuerte y fresca. Los efectos del aceite de romero son térmicos, estimulantes, fortalecedores y tonificantes para cuerpo y mente.

Las propiedades analgésicas de este aceite hacen que sea útil en el tratamiento de dolores por migraña, y sus propiedades estimulantes ayudan a devolver la concentración y revitalizar el ánimo, particularmente cuando hay fatiga por trabajo excesivo.

Este aceite puede usarse en el baño, con masajes o para aromatizar una habitación.

En una dilución de 1%, el aceite de romero es bastante seguro. Debe evitarse durante el embarazo. No es conveniente para quien padece de epilepsia o presión alta.

Para que la aromaterapia sea efectiva, los aceites esenciales siempre deben provenir de fuentes naturales. Los extractos sintéticos no sólo no producen el mismo efecto, sino que pueden producir reacciones negativas. Así es que sea muy cuidadoso a la hora de comprar sus aceites. Adquiéralos en pequeñas cantidades, ya que entre más se abra una botella y se exponga al aire, más fácilmente perderá sus cualidades.

Almacénelos en un lugar fresco y oscuro. Por lo general, los aceites esenciales duran de uno a dos años, pero si ya están mezclados con los aceites base no debe utilizarlos por más de tres meses.

Musicoterapia

La musicoterapia es el uso de la música para mejorar el funcionamiento físico, psicológico, intelectual o social de personas que tienen problemas de salud o educativos.

La musicoterapia puede ser definida como: "...un proceso de intervención sistemática, en el cual el terapeuta ayuda al paciente a obtener la salud a través de experiencias musicales y de las relaciones que se desarrollan a través de ellas como las fuerzas dinámicas para el cambio".

La musicoterapia se puede utilizar con niños, adultos y personas de la tercera edad con diferentes problemas físicos, emocionales, intelectuales o sociales.

También se emplea con personas que no están enfermas o que no tienen algún problema, para mejorar el bienestar personal, desarrollar la creatividad, mejorar el aprendizaje y las relaciones interpersonales, así como para el manejo del estrés.

En los niños se usa para mejorar la autoestima, la atención y concentración, la coordinación, el aprendizaje y la socialización, entre otras.

La musicoterapia busca descubrir potenciales y/o restituir funciones del individuo para que éste alcance una mejor organización intra y/o interpersonal y, consecuentemente, una mejor calidad de vida a través de la prevención y rehabilitación en un tratamiento.

Los orígenes de la musicoterapia tal vez sean tan antiguos como los hombres primitivos que danzaban para invocar a los espíritus curativos; sin embargo, esta práctica se comenzó a popularizar en los años sesenta, cuando las investigaciones comprobaron el éxito de esta terapia al ser utilizada para tratar pacientes catatónicos.

Actualmente, la musicoterapia se utiliza en la medicina, la psicoterapia y en la educación especial como práctica auxiliar en diversos tratamientos.

En el caso de la migraña, la música ayuda a disminuir el dolor, ya que ayuda a la producción de endorfinas que actúan como calmantes naturales del dolor. Además, el escuchar música ayuda a la relajación.

Si durante sus ataques de migraña no experimenta fonofobia (sensibilidad extrema al ruido), intente relajarse escuchando algo de música de su agrado.

La *Serenata* de Schubert, el *Sueño de amor* de Liszt o música que reproduzca los sonidos de la naturaleza, pueden ser excelentes opciones para relajarse; sin embargo, cualquier música tranquila que a usted le guste puede servir para ese propósito.

Utilice la música como terapia complementaria para aliviar sus dolores de migraña.

Masajes

El masaje es un recurso instintivo para reconfortar. Entre los animales, las madres frotan a sus crías y los adultos de muchas especies se soban unos a otros. El masaje es la forma de tratamiento curativo más antiguo de todas las culturas.

En las últimas dos décadas, una serie de estudios científicos ha corroborado lo que se venía asegurando desde la antigüedad: el masaje es una terapia beneficiosa, no sólo para relajar sino también para aliviar muchas alteraciones, desde la migraña hasta la depresión o la sinusitis.

Hipócrates, el padre de la medicina, escribió: "Los médicos tienen que ser expertos en muchas cosas, pero especialmente en anatripsia, el arte de la fricción, porque el masaje puede ajustar una articulación que esté demasiado suelta o relajar otra que esté demasiado rígida".

Hipócrates enseñaba a sus alumnos cómo manipular el cuerpo de sus pacientes para aliviar los problemas circulatorios y de las articulaciones.

El masaje es tan antiguo como el ser humano. Frotar la piel para sanar es un instinto tan natural como respirar, pero su uso como tratamiento no siempre ha sido aceptado y respetado por la comunidad científica.

Con el tiempo, el masaje en Occidente acabó considerándose un pasatiempo frívolo de las clases más adineradas. Sin embargo, en los últimos años se está produciendo una avalancha de nuevos adeptos a las técnicas del masaje. ¿El motivo? Más de cien estudios corroboran lo que ya se sugería en los textos chinos hace más de 3 mil años: el masaje es eficaz para combatir enfermedades tan diversas como la migraña, la depresión, la artritis o el asma.

El mayor avance del masaje terapéutico no se ha observado en la técnica, que ha seguido siendo prácticamente la misma a lo largo del último siglo, sino en la publicación de las investigaciones que confirman y explican cuáles son sus beneficios médicos.

Acariciar, frotar, palmear, pellizcar, presionar, teclear y hacer vibrar ciertas partes del cuerpo logra objetivos que, a veces, ni la medicina de alta tecnología es capaz de conseguir. Mejora la función del sistema inmune, aumenta el nivel de endorfinas, acelera la recuperación física, disminuye la tensión arterial y alivia la depresión y la ansiedad.

En la sociedad actual, en la que las alteraciones psicológicas y fisiológicas causadas por el estrés son las más frecuentes, el masaje empieza a representar un papel importante para proporcionar relajación y bienestar y para mantener una buena salud. Las investigaciones han mostrado, por ejemplo, que reduce la tasa cardiaca y la presión arterial, estimula el flujo linfático y sanguíneo, relaja los músculos, mejora la capacidad de movilidad y aumenta la liberación de endorfinas.

Un masaje a la semana para liberar la tensión puede ser lo único que necesite para evitar los dolores de migraña, cuando éstos son ocasionados por el estrés. Sin embargo, es importante que elija a un terapeuta calificado que sepa manejar las técnicas adecuadas, ya que, como ocurre con cualquier otro tratamiento, escoger una técnica equivocada puede que no cause efecto o, lo que es peor, que cause un efecto perjudicial.

Los masajistas calificados siguen una enseñanza que incluye clases de anatomía, fisiología, técnicas y ejercicios para dar agilidad a las manos, códigos de ética, contraindicaciones del masaje, primeros auxilios, etcétera.

Existen distintas modalidades de masaje, cada una de ellas con una manera propia de relajar, aunque todas ellas están encaminadas a relajar la tensión muscular y a mejorar la circulación linfática.

El profesional debe saber escoger y aplicar las distintas técnicas para conseguir el tratamiento adecuado, aunque el efecto terapéutico no depende sólo de la técnica sino de la habilidad del masajista y de lo receptivo que esté el paciente.

Los suaves movimientos que acarician, amasan, frotan y golpetean la piel, muchas veces combinados con el empleo de aceites aromáticos, liberan a los músculos de la tensión, relajan las articulaciones, mejoran la circulación y eliminan las toxinas acumuladas.

La técnica más conocida es la de masaje sueco, ésta fue desarrollada en Suecia a principios del siglo XIX por Per Henrik Ling. Para este tipo de masaje, la persona se desviste y se tiende sobre una mesa acojinada, mientras el terapeuta queda de pie. Una toalla o sábana cubre las zonas del cuerpo que no reciben masaje. Se vierte aceite tibio sobre la piel, que después se frota de diversas maneras. Dependiendo de la frotación, se usan los dedos, las palmas o los bordes de las manos, los pulgares, codos y antebrazos. La mayoría de las veces, el masaje es suave y placentero. Sin embargo, cuando es profundo, los músculos se estimulan y oprimen con energía. El efecto debe ser tonificante y no desagradable.

Siga las siguientes recomendaciones:

✓ Absténgase del masaje sueco de cuerpo completo en el momento del dolor de migraña. Durante el dolor, existen masajes que se puede dar usted mismo: Aplique masaje en la parte posterior del cuello, las sienes, el cuero cabelludo y la cara. Haga que se relajen esos músculos y así logrará disminuir o desaparecer el dolor de migraña ocasionado por la tensión.

✓ Evite el masaje directo sobre alguna herida, hematoma, quemadura, incisión o sobre alguna vena varicosa, infección cutánea o ronchas.

✓ Evite los masajistas que anuncian sus servicios en los clasificados.

Si usted no quiere recurrir a un masajista profesional por cualquier razón, una excelente opción es que, junto con su pareja, aprenda algunas técnicas de masaje; así, además de relajar la tensión, el darse masajes mutuos los acercará más como pareja.

Técnicas de masaje

Fricción

La fricción se usa mucho en el masaje y es un movimiento que se realiza de manera sencilla. Básicamente, la fricción es un tipo de palmadas, variando la presión a seguir y usando toda la mano. Usar la fricción para iniciar el masaje es una buena opción, ya que relaja a la persona y, si utiliza aceites esenciales para el masaje, éstos se comenzarán a esparcir sobre una superficie grande de la piel desde un principio y empezarán a actuar. Hay que comenzar suavemente, trabajando en dirección del corazón todo el tiempo para fomentar el retorno venoso. Mantenga las palmadas suaves y continuas. La presión debe ser fuerte sin llegar a lastimar.

Frotación y amasamiento

La frotación es la técnica adecuada para áreas donde no hay bastante piel; por ejemplo, donde la piel esté muy pegada a los huesos. El amasamiento se utiliza en áreas más carnosas, como en los muslos o brazos. Use las yemas de los dedos y la eminencia tenar (montículo) de los pulgares para la frotación, moviendo en círculos alrededor de las áreas reducidas de la piel. Hágalo en dirección de las manecillas del reloj con la mano derecha y en sentido contrario con la mano izquierda. No deslice las manos sobre la piel como en la fricción, más bien mueva la piel, un área reducida a la vez, por los dedos y los pulgares.

El amasamiento se realiza con los dedos y los pulgares rectos, levantando un área de la piel y pasándola a la otra mano. La presión debe ser fuerte pero no dolorosa.

La fricción y el amasamiento estimulan la circulación sanguínea.

Masaje de espalda

Cuando dé masaje de espalda, hágalo utilizando el método de la fricción, trabajando con una mano de cada lado de la columna. Trabaje de la parte inferior de la columna hacia arriba dando palmadas ascendentes; al llegar a los hombros, el movimiento se debe hacer hacia fuera. Este masaje resulta muy relajante. Mantenga las manos sobre la persona y siga rodeando por los hombros, bajando por los costados de la persona hacia la cintura.

Haga movimientos suaves y fluidos; cuando quite una mano de la espalda, la otra debe de permanecer en contacto. Trabaje ambos lados de la columna usando la fricción, haciendo pequeños movimientos circulares con los pulgares mientras mueve las manos hacia arriba, desde la región lumbar hasta el cuello.

Mientras se trabaja en el masaje, es posible detectar nudos de tensión específicos sobre los que debe poner más atención. Al terminar el masaje, antes de que la persona se levante debe descansar un momento.

Masaje de cuello y hombros

Es maravilloso para aliviar la migraña ocasionada por tensión y estrés. No es necesario que la persona esté acostada, puede estar sentada.

Use la fricción dando palmadas en dirección contraria a las manecillas del reloj; trabaje rodeando de los hombros al cuello. Frote el cuello a ambos lados de la columna, trabajando de la base del cuello hacia arriba para soltar los nudos de tensión. Con las palmas de las manos encima de los hombros de la persona, trabaje en círculos con los pulgares alrededor de las áreas más carnosas y empuje con movimientos ascendentes. Termine el masaje con fricción en los hombros.

Masaje de cara

Éste debe de ser muy suave; cubra los ojos de la persona con algodón antes de comenzar. Use la fricción dando palmadas suaves del centro de la cara hacia fuera.

Comience debajo del mentón, trabaje hacia fuera de las orejas, después del centro de la cara por la nariz hacia arriba y hacia fuera a las sienes. Palmee hacia fuera del centro de la frente hacia las sienes. Presione con más firmeza en los lados de las sienes. Este masaje es adecuado para aplicarse durante el dolor de migraña en su fase inicial, siempre y cuando no resulte molesto para la persona.

Estos masajes se pueden complementar con aromaterapia para mejorar sus resultados.

Así es que si usted cree que los masajes son tan sólo una frivolidad, haga la prueba, no pierde nada, un masaje corto de unos 15 minutos puede liberarlo del estrés que acumula toda la semana en el trabajo a consecuencia de malas posturas, presiones por fechas de entrega y conflictos con sus compañeros de trabajo.

Técnicas de relajación

El estrés y el consumo de ciertos alimentos son los disparadores más frecuentes de la migraña; como ya los habíamos mencionado, es relativamente sencillo controlar lo que comemos, pero resulta casi imposible alejarnos de las situaciones que nos producen estrés.

El estrés es un fenómeno de adaptación al medio. Es un conjunto de reacciones ante un estímulo que en ocasiones puede salvarnos la vida y en otras, dañarla (estrés positivo y negativo).

Hay tres etapas en la respuesta del estrés:

1. **Alarma:** el cuerpo reconoce el estímulo y se prepara liberando hormonas que aumentan los latidos, la glucosa en el torrente sanguíneo, la frecuencia respiratoria, la transpiración, etc. Éstas son reacciones que nos preparan para enfrentar el peligro o para huir del mismo.
2. **Resistencia:** el cuerpo intenta reparar el daño producido por la reacción de alarma. Si el estrés

continúa, el cuerpo permanece alerta y no puede reparar los daños. Continúa la resistencia y se pasa a la tercera etapa.

3. **Agotamiento:** va desde el simple agotamiento de las reservas hasta situaciones extremas como la muerte.

Vivimos en una sociedad con muchas amenazas presentes casi todo el tiempo y en la que se le da prioridad a los logros económicos más que a los espirituales.

A su vez, algunas personas tienden a ser más sensibles y a producir una descarga de hormonas exagerada y sostenida en el tiempo, que produce una menor calidad y cantidad de vida.

Sin embargo, es posible aprender técnicas de relajación que lograrán controlar nuestro estrés y, gracias a ello, eliminar las consecuencias negativas que éste puede traer a nuestro organismo; entre ellas, los dolores de migraña.

Las técnicas de relajación actúan sobre el sistema nervioso para que éste modifique el estado de estrés de nuestro organismo, regresando a niveles de normalidad; es decir, si el estrés está provocando una respiración agitada, transpiración excesiva y un rápido palpitar del corazón, gracias a la relajación nuestro organismo volverá a sus ritmos normales.

La respiración profunda es la técnica más sencilla de relajación. Seguramente muchas veces, cuando usted ha estado alterado, alguien le habrá dicho: "cálmese y respire tranquilo"; pues esta sugerencia puede ser de gran ayuda para lograr eliminar el estrés y, con ello, ahorrarse un dolor de cabeza.

Técnica de respiración profunda

1. Escoja un espacio tranquilo (puede ser una habitación de su casa en la que se pueda aislar del ruido), desconecte el teléfono, pida a su familia que no lo moleste y deje la habitación en penumbras.
2. Utilice ropa cómoda, quítese reloj, pulseras, anillos, lentes (incluso de contacto); siéntase libre y ligero.
3. Siéntese cómodamente en una silla o sillón.
4. Cierre los ojos y comience a tomar conciencia de su respiración.

5. Aspire por la nariz lenta y profundamente desde el diafragma. Notará que su estómago sube y baja.
6. Concéntrese únicamente en su respiración. No piense en nada más que inhalar y exhalar. Si acuden a su mente pensamientos que lo distraen, intente pensar en un punto blanco o imagine una estrella única en el firmamento. Concéntrese en ello y siga con la respiración.
7. Siga así por 20 minutos.
8. Abra los ojos lentamente y regrese a su respiración normal. Se sentirá relajado y el estrés y el dolor habrán desaparecido.

Una vez que domine esta técnica, le resultará sencillo realizarla durante un pequeño descanso en su trabajo o en el auto mientras se estaciona por unos minutos. Además, logrará asimilar mejor cualquier situación estresante, simplemente respirando profundamente desde el diafragma con los ojos cerrados por unos cuantos segundos.

Relajación muscular progresiva

Esta técnica consta de dos fases.

a) En la primera fase se aprende a discriminar cuando un músculo está tenso y cuando está relajado. Para ello, estando en una posición cómoda, tumbado o recostado, hay que tensar cada músculo y después de mantenerlo tenso durante tres o cuatro segundos, relajarlo. Hay que centrarse en la sensación de relajación y en la diferencia entre ésta y la anterior sensación de tensión.

Los grupos musculares que suelen trabajarse en esta primera fase, son los siguientes:

Manos: apriete los puños; primero uno y luego el otro.

Antebrazos: doble los brazos por el codo y apriete el antebrazo contra el brazo; primero un lado, después el otro.

Brazos: ponga los brazos rectos, con las manos sueltas y estiradas hacia delante; primero un lado, luego el otro.

Hombros: levántelos hacia arriba; primero un lado, después el otro.

Nuca: apriete la barbilla contra el pecho y luego contra la superficie en la que está reposando.

Frente: levante las cejas hacia arriba y arrugue la frente.

Ojos: apriete los párpados.

Boca: ábrala lo más posible y después apriete los labios.

Mandíbulas: ténselas.

Lengua: apriete la punta de la lengua contra la parte superior del paladar.

Pecho: tome aire por la nariz, manteniéndolo mientras se tensa el pecho y soltándolo lentamente por la boca.

Abdomen: empuje fuertemente los músculos abdominales.

Nalgas: ténselas y empújelas hacia arriba junto con las caderas.

Muslos: extienda las piernas, levántelas y estírelas.

Pantorrillas: extienda las piernas hacia fuera, enderece y tense los dedos de los pies.

Pies: mueva los dedos hacia abajo y después hacia arriba.

Durante el ejercicio, hay que ir tomando el tiempo para centrar la atención en cada uno de los grupos musculares, notando la diferencia entre la sensación de tensión y de relajamiento. Aproximadamente unos siete segundos por cada parte del cuerpo.

La respiración debe de ser pausada y a través del diafragma. Notará que está haciendo la respiración adecuada cuando su estómago suba y baje.

Para aprender a relajarse, es importante mantener una actitud de atención pasiva y no tener prisa. Al empezar, se debe practicar en un lugar silencioso, con temperatura agradable y una posición corporal cómoda: tumbado o sentado en un sillón.

b) En la segunda fase, una vez que haya aprendido a discriminar fácilmente cualquier tensión muscular y a relajarla a voluntad, hay que prestar atención al cuerpo para distinguir cualquier músculo tenso y poder trabajar en relajarlo. Para ello, hay que revisar mentalmente cada zona o grupo muscular y relajar cualquier tensión que se detecte en ella, sin necesidad de tensarlas antes.

Ya que se domine esta técnica de relajación muscular, intente realizarla de pie, mientras camina, mientras habla con alguien o mientras está en su oficina.

La práctica de la relajación para afrontar la ansiedad en las situaciones interpersonales implica ser capaz de ocupar en ella una parte de su atención, mientras deja libre otra parte de su mente para atender otras tareas.

Estas técnicas le ayudarán a relajarse; sin embargo, hay muchas cosas sencillas que usted puede hacer en su vida diaria que le ayudarán a eliminar o evitar el estrés al enfrentarse a problemas mayores:

- ✓ Levántese más temprano.
- ✓ Prepare su ropa la noche anterior.
- ✓ Planee sus citas con tiempo.
- ✓ Lleve una agenda.
- ✓ Haga un duplicado de las llaves.
- ✓ Decida prioridades en su vida.
- ✓ Cuando sea necesario, diga NO.
- ✓ Evite el trato con personas negativas.
- ✓ Haga copias de sus documentos importantes.
- ✓ Repare cualquier cosa que no esté funcionando adecuadamente.

- ✓ Divida las grandes tareas en pequeñas porciones de trabajo.
- ✓ Sonría.
- ✓ Trate de ver los problemas como retos.
- ✓ Esté preparado para las inclemencias del clima.
- ✓ Haga reír a un bebé.
- ✓ Acaricie una mascota.
- ✓ Dígale algo amable a alguien.
- ✓ Tenga su coche en buenas condiciones.
- ✓ Juegue con un niño.
- ✓ Camine de vez en cuando bajo la lluvia.
- ✓ Reserve todos los días en su agenda un momento sólo para usted.
- ✓ Tome un relajante baño de tina.
- ✓ Sea consciente de las decisiones que toma.
- ✓ Crea en sí mismo.
- ✓ Deje de decir cosas negativas.
- ✓ Véase a sí mismo triunfando.
- ✓ Mantenga su sentido del humor.
- ✓ Aléjese de amistades destructivas.
- ✓ Tenga metas en la vida.
- ✓ Abrace a sus seres queridos.
- ✓ Túmbese en un jardín y vea las estrellas.

- ✓ Cante, aunque sea en la regadera.
- ✓ También baile.
- ✓ Acurrúquese en la cama con su pareja.
- ✓ Intente algo nuevo.
- ✓ Tome un día a la vez.
- ✓ Tómese un tiempo para disfrutar de un jardín, admire la belleza de las flores, huélalas.
- ✓ Tenga siempre un plan B.
- ✓ Duerma lo suficiente.
- ✓ Esfuércese por ser optimista.
- ✓ Mantenga su peso.
- ✓ Busque momentos románticos con su pareja.
- ✓ Platique con sus hijos.
- ✓ Tenga a la mano los teléfonos de las personas que le pueden ayudar a salir de un problema.
- ✓ Busque hacer nuevos amigos.
- ✓ Vaya al futbol y grite.
- ✓ Vaya al ballet o a un concierto de música clásica y disfrútelo.
- ✓ Prepare una cena especial y compártala con sus amigos.
- ✓ Cene a la luz de las velas con su pareja.
- ✓ Haga ejercicio.

- ✓ Vea una caricatura que lo haga reír.
- ✓ Coma su platillo favorito.
- ✓ Váyase de vacaciones.
- ✓ Conozca un lugar nuevo.
- ✓ Ahorre para los gastos imprevistos.
- ✓ Pídale a alguien de su confianza que cuide a sus hijos para pasar una velada a solas con su pareja.
- ✓ Permanezca enamorado.
- ✓ ¡DISFRUTE LA VIDA!

Ejercicio

Si usted constantemente se ve torturado por los dolores de cabeza por migraña, lo mejor que puede hacer es comenzar a hacer ejercicio.

El ejercicio, además de ser una maravillosa forma de evitar las tensiones, ayuda de otra manera: nuestro cerebro secreta unas hormonas que se llaman endorfinas, éstas son los analgésicos naturales del cuerpo; sin embargo, cuando padecemos de un dolor crónico, las endorfinas se agotan y una de las maneras de secretar más es por medio del ejercicio.

Eso que nos hace sentirnos muy bien después de una hora de haber hecho ejercicio son las endorfinas, que logran que cambie nuestro estado de ánimo y que toleremos mejor el dolor.

Realizar ejercicio físico es una actividad indispensable para reducir los ataques de migraña; además, puede resultar muy gratificante tanto desde el punto de vista físico como psicológico.

Entre los beneficios para la salud fisiológica y psicológica que supone el ejercicio, se encuentran los siguientes:

Fisiológicos

Efectos inmediatos.

1. Contribuye a la regulación de:
   a) El nivel de glucosa.
   b) El nivel de algunos transmisores nerviosos para el funcionamiento correcto del cuerpo.
   c) Estimula la noradrenalina y la adrenalina.
   d) Potencia la elaboración de endorfinas.
   e) Mejora el sueño.

Efectos a largo plazo.

1. Sensación de bienestar físico, de "estar en forma".
   a) Fortalecimiento de los sistemas cardiovascular y respiratorio, incrementando la cantidad de oxígeno que llega a los diferentes órganos y tejidos corporales. Mejora general del funcionamiento de estos sistemas.

b) Incremento de la resistencia muscular, con los consiguientes efectos benéficos sobre la autonomía personal.

c) Favorece:
   - La agilidad y flexibilidad corporal.
   - El equilibrio y la coordinación.
   - La rapidez de movimientos, previniendo y retrasando la aparición de los declives asociados a la edad en estas funciones.

Psicológicos

Efectos inmediatos.

1. Relajación.
2. Mejora del estado de ánimo.
3. Disminuye el estrés y la ansiedad.

Efectos a largo plazo.

1. Bienestar psicológico general.
2. Mejora la autoimagen de la persona.
3. Favorece la sensación de control sobre la propia vida.
4. Potencia el funcionamiento cognitivo e intelectual.
5. Favorece la psicomotricidad.

Los dolores de migraña a menudo están relacionados con los dolores en el cuello, para lo que recomendamos el siguiente ejercicio:

- ✓ Colóquese las palmas de las manos en la frente y empuje hacia atrás; presione hacia adelante con la cabeza para resistir la presión de las manos, hágalo seis segundos.
- ✓ Colóquese las palmas de las manos en la nuca y haga presión con la cabeza durante 6 segundos.
- ✓ Repita el ejercicio hacia el lado izquierdo y derecho de la cabeza, seis segundos cada vez.

Con este ejercicio se hace resistencia con los músculos del cuello y, como consecuencia, se fortalecen.

El estrés y la actividad física están íntimamente relacionados. Cuando hacemos ejercicio nos sentimos mejor, más descargados de las tensiones cotidianas y con los ánimos renovados. El ejercicio que viene a continuación puede ser una buena solución para eliminar las tensiones físicas y mentales que acumulamos en la vida diaria.

El ejercicio dura alrededor de 10 minutos y es suficiente con hacerlo dos veces al día. Se divide en diferentes fases pero no debe olvidar que el ejercicio es uno y lo más importante al principio es fluir con la energía que se genera.

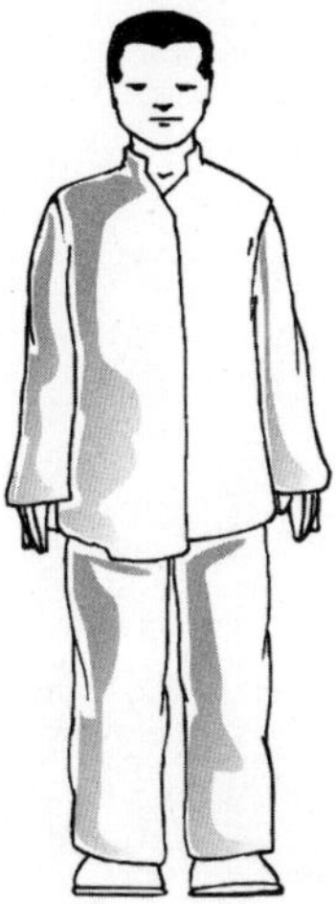

Postura básica

En posición de pie con los brazos relajados junto al cuerpo y las palmas de las manos mirando atrás para abrir el pecho de manera natural.

La cabeza descansa en el tronco, el pecho en el abdomen, la cadera en las rodillas y todo el peso de la cabeza se descarga por las plantas de los pies.

Del mismo modo, descargamos todos los pensamientos, emociones y deseos.

Los dejamos ir, simplemente sonriendo desde el corazón.

Inicio del ejercicio

1. Llevamos las palmas de las manos al frente paralelas al suelo (los dedos de cada mano se apuntan entre sí) y levantamos los brazos por delante hasta llevarlos por encima de la cabeza, como si levantáramos el cielo con las palmas.

Los ojos siguen a las manos hasta arriba.

Mientras realizamos este movimiento, inspiramos suavemente por la nariz, sin forzar la respiración.

2. Empujamos el cielo desde los pies. Al llegar las palmas arriba, empujamos el cielo desde la planta de los pies, sin tensar los hombros. La cabeza se echa un poco hacia atrás.

Cada vez que empuje las palmas hacia el cielo, sienta cómo se le endereza la espalda.

En este momento, hay una pequeña pausa respiratoria de uno o dos segundos.

3. Bajamos los brazos desde los hombros.

Después de empujar el cielo, dejamos que los brazos caigan la ambos lados del cuerpo hasta que las palmas de las manos toquen la parte superior de las piernas. Sienta cómo baja el flujo de energía por su cuerpo.

Mientras bajamos los brazos exhalamos, sacando el aire suavemente por la boca.

Hacemos una ligera pausa antes de inspirar y comenzamos de nuevo el ejercicio según la figura (a), hasta completar una serie de 12 movimientos.

Disfrutamos del movimiento espontáneo

4. Después de haber realizado 12 veces los pasos a, b y c, es decir, después de 12 respiraciones, nos quedamos en el sitio sin hacer algún movimiento consciente, para disfrutar el fluir espontáneo del cuerpo que se manifiesta en pequeños movimientos como balanceos, espirales, giros, etcétera.

Este momento es el más importante de todos para expulsar el estrés. Es necesario que nos relajemos y disfrutemos del no-hacer; de lo contrario, si por ejemplo tensamos las piernas o los brazos, el estrés acumulado no se eliminará.

Al principio, si nota rigidez o dificultad para soltarse, puede balancear suavemente la pelvis, eso le ayudará a relajarse.

Disfrutamos de la quietud

5. Después de estar de cinco a 10 minutos eliminando tensiones y bloqueos a través de los movimientos espontáneos, concéntrese por debajo del ombligo y disfrute de la quietud física y mental.

En esta posición puede estar unos cinco minutos.

Luego, frote sus manos y dese un masaje por los ojos, frente, sienes, nuca y cuello.

Para terminar, camine unos pasos con energía.

Observaciones

Comience haciendo el ejercicio 12 veces, luego disfrute del movimiento espontáneo y termine disfrutando de la calma física y mental.

Poco a poco puede alargar la serie de movimientos hasta 24 veces, más adelante hasta 36..., pero recuerde que lo más importante es el punto 4, disfrutar del movimiento espontáneo, para desbloquear su organismo y recuperar su salud y su fuerza vital.

Es muy importante que respire con suavidad. Un error muy común al principio es forzar la respiración y lo que se consigue con esto es aumentar la tensión.

No cierre la boca, manténgala relajada, sonriendo desde el corazón; de este modo y con la ayuda de la exhalación, eliminará el estrés más rápidamente.

Practique todos los días.

La migraña también puede ser ocasionada por la falta de sueño; si ése es su caso, siga las siguientes recomendaciones de ejercicio para eliminar el insomnio.

El ejercicio terapéutico recomendado para el insomnio incluye las siguientes actividades:

1. Caminata, durante por lo menos media hora, una vez al día, todos los días.

2. Se recomienda también la práctica diaria de algún deporte, como:
   a) Natación.
   b) Ciclismo.
   c) Gimnasia al aire libre.
   d) Ejercicios respiratorios y de relajamiento físico y mental.

3. Los siguientes ejercicios calisténicos:

Giros de cuello.

1. Rote la cabeza hacia la derecha.
2. Ruede el mentón a lo largo del pecho hacia la izquierda.

Giros de hombros.

1. Gire los hombros hacia atrás en círculos amplios.
2. Apoye las manos en los hombros y realice círculos.

Hacer ejercicio le ayudará a disminuir los dolores de migraña, pero además le aportará muchos otros beneficios. Las personas que realizan una actividad física regular, de intensidad moderada y por lo menos tres veces por semana o si es posible todos los días, viven más años y tienen una mejor calidad de vida. Es recomendable realizar natación, trote, caminata, bicicleta, etcétera.

Elija la actividad que más le guste para que así la realice por placer y no por obligación; si padece de alguna enfermedad, si nunca en su vida ha realizado más ejercicio que el que hacía en la secundaria o si tiene más de 35 años, consulte a su médico para saber cuál es el ejercicio que más le conviene dependiendo de sus características.

Terapia alimenticia

Nuestra alimentación está estrechamente relacionada con la aparición de los dolores de migraña; sin embargo, resulta casi imposible determinar el número de episodios de migraña vinculados con los alimentos, ya que en algunos casos es la causa principal del dolor, pero en otros es la combinación de varios factores, que pueden ser alimenticios, físicos y psicológicos, lo que puede desencadenar el dolor.

La razón por la que algunos alimentos desencadenan dolores de migraña se debe a algunas sustancias químicas contenidas en ellos, en especial tiraminas y nitrito.

Estas sustancias ejercen un efecto directo sobre el cerebro, provocando cambios vasculares y neurales que terminan en dolor de cabeza.

En algunos casos, los alimentos estimulan la constricción de los vasos sanguíneos, provocando molestias visuales; en otros, los vasos sanguíneos se dilatan, ocasionando dolor.

Por otra parte, también existen alimentos que afectan los cambios vasculares y los procesos inflamatorios del cerebro por lo que pueden ayudar a aliviar el dolor de cabeza.

Lo que es un hecho es que eliminando de nuestra dieta, o al menos reduciendo al mínimo, el consumo de los alimentos que contienen tiraminas y nitrito, podemos reducir en gran medida los episodios de migraña.

La siguiente es una dieta que mantiene los niveles de tiramina y nitrito al mínimo:

Bebidas

- ✓ Alimentos permitidos: café descafeinado, jugos de fruta, agua mineral, refrescos sin cola.
- ✓ Alimentos a evitarse: café, té negro, refrescos de cola, chocolate caliente, bebidas alcohólicas.

Productos lácteos

- ✓ Alimentos permitidos: leche homogeneizada, semidescremada o descremada. Queso panela, fresco, americano, requesón, ricotta, queso crema, yogur (sólo una porción al día).

- ✓ Alimentos a evitarse: productos lácteos cultivados como suero de leche, crema ácida, leche con chocolate. Quesos: azul, brie, camembert, cheddar, suizo, gouda, roquefort, mozzarella, parmesano, provolone, emmental.

Carnes, pescados y aves

- ✓ Alimentos permitidos: pavo, pollo, pescado, carne de res, cordero, ternera y cerdo frescos o congelados; huevos (sólo tres por semana), atún.
- ✓ Alimentos a evitarse: carnes enlatadas, curadas, añejadas o procesadas, como jamón enlatado, arenque en vinagre, pescado salado, hígado de pollo, salchichas, salami, pepperoni; cualquier carne preparada con ablandador, salsa de soya o extractos de levadura.

Panes y cereales

- ✓ Alimentos permitidos: panes comerciales como el blanco, de trigo integral, centeno, francés, italiano, muffins, tostadas melba, galletas de soda. Todos los cereales calientes y fríos. Hojuelas de maíz, hojaldre de trigo, arroz, salvado.

- ✓ Alimentos a evitarse: panes con levadura, panes y galletas que contengan queso, donas, panes de masa ácida, todos los panes y cereales que contengan chocolate o nueces.

Almidones

- ✓ Alimentos permitidos: papas, arroz, macarrones, espaguetis, fideos.

Verduras, legumbres y semillas

- ✓ Alimentos permitidos: espárragos, col, zanahoria, calabaza, espinaca, tomates, calabacín, calabaza italiana, brócoli, lechuga, todos a excepción de los señalados en el siguiente párrafo.
- ✓ Alimentos a evitarse: habas, lentejas, habas verdes, frijoles blancos, bayos o pintos; chícharos de vaina, col ácida, garbanzos, cebollas (excepto como condimento), aceitunas, encurtidos, cacahuates, semillas de girasol, de ajonjolí o de calabaza.

Frutas

- ✓ Alimentos permitidos: ciruelas, manzanas, cerezas, duraznos, peras. Frutas cítricas y jugos: limítese a media taza por día de naranja, toronja, mandarina, piña, lima o limón.
- ✓ Alimentos a evitarse: aguacates, plátanos (medio plátano por día), higos, uvas, pasas, papaya, fruta de la pasión, ciruelas rojas.

Sopas

- ✓ Alimentos permitidos: sopas tipo crema elaboradas con los alimentos señalados antes como permitidos; caldos hechos en casa.
- ✓ Alimentos a evitarse: sopas enlatadas, cubitos concentrados de caldo, bases para sopa con levadura o glutamato monosódico (consulte las etiquetas).

Postres

- ✓ Alimentos permitidos: las frutas mencionadas anteriormente en helados, gelatinas, pasteles y galletas que no contengan chocolate, nueces o levadura.

- ✓ Alimentos a evitarse: helados, pasteles o galletas con chocolate.

Golosinas

- ✓ Alimentos permitidos: azúcar, jalea, mermelada, miel, caramelos duros.
- ✓ Alimentos a evitarse: dulces de chocolate, jarabe de chocolate.

Varios

- ✓ Alimentos permitidos: sal (con moderación), jugo de limón, mantequilla o margarina, aceites para cocinar, crema para batir, vinagre blanco y aderezos comerciales para ensaladas en cantidades pequeñas.
- ✓ Alimentos a evitarse: pizza, salsa de queso, salsa de soya, glutamato monosódico, levadura, extracto de levadura, sal de sazonar, cenas congeladas, cualquier comida encurtida, conservada o marinada.

Existen ciertos alimentos que son los que tienen la peor reputación por ser desencadenantes de migrañas, estos son:

Vino tinto

No sólo ocasiona dolor por su contenido de alcohol y por la resaca que puede ocasionar después de consumirlo en exceso. La principal causa que lo hace enemigo de los pacientes con migraña es su alto contenido de tiramina, entre otras sustancias que ocasionan cambios vasculares.

Chocolate

Éste es tristemente famoso por ser el segundo alimento que más ocasiona dolores de migraña. El primero es el alcohol. Al igual que el vino tinto, el chocolate tiene un alto contenido de tiramina. Sin embargo, esta sustancia no está presente en el chocolate blanco que contiene manteca de cacao, pero no licor de chocolate, por lo cual puede ser consumido.

Salchicha

Al igual que el tocino, el jamón y el salami, contiene nitrito o nitrato de sodio. Tenga especial cuidado en las dietas de los niños, ya que son los que más consumen las salchichas.

Aspartame

No se conoce la razón por la cual el aspartame puede desencadenar dolores de cabeza, pero ciertos estudios han comprobado que en una gran cantidad de personas que sufren de migraña, los dolores cesan cuando dejan de consumir aspartame. Además, las migrañas ocasionadas por este edulcorante suelen presentarse con mareos, debilidad y visión borrosa. Revise las etiquetas de los productos que compra, ya que podría estar consumiendo aspartame sin darse cuenta.

Glutamato monosódico

Esta sustancia se utiliza generalmente para realzar los sabores de los alimentos procesados (consulte las etiquetas) y se encuentra siempre en la comida china.

Esta sustancia desencadena dolores de migraña en personas que no la metabolizan bien, de manera que se va acumulando en la corriente sanguínea produciendo una reacción química que provoca los dolores.

Cafeína

Si bien es cierto que la cafeína es un analgésico que puede aliviar el dolor de cabeza de manera temporal al contraer los vasos sanguíneos dilatados, a la larga, consumirla tiene sus consecuencias.

Cuando el efecto inmediato de la cafeína desaparece, los vasos contraídos se dilatan todavía más, empeorando la migraña.

Sin embargo, para alguien que está acostumbrado a consumir cafeína y no la obtiene, la abstinencia puede también provocar dolores de cabeza además de fatiga, depresión leve, dolor, náusea, vómito y rigidez. Lo recomendable para eliminar esta sustancia de su dieta que está contenida en el café y en algunos refrescos, es dejarla poco a poco en un lapso de dos semanas.

Por otra parte, existen alimentos que pueden ayudar a curar los dolores ocasionados por la migraña, éstos son:

Pescado y aceite de pescado

Consumir pescado con regularidad, especialmente el de tipo grasoso, como el salmón, atún y sardinas, produce efectos de largo plazo sobre la química cerebral, contribuyendo a reducir con el tiempo los ataques de migraña.

Para reducir sus ataques de migraña, puede tomar cápsulas de aceite de pescado durante seis semanas y después incrementar en su dieta el consumo de pescado.

Jengibre

Esta planta ha sido utilizada por siglos para aliviar los dolores de cabeza. El jengibre afecta las prostaglandinas, sustancias de tipo hormonal que ayudan a controlar las respuestas inflamatorias del organismo. El jengibre reduce la inflamación y, por consiguiente, el dolor. Pruebe consumir un tercio de cucharadita de jengibre en polvo al día como parte de su dieta.

Magnesio

El magnesio es un elemento esencial que juega un papel muy importante en las migrañas. Muchos casos de migraña se asocian con bajos niveles de magnesio.

Recientemente se han realizado estudios que han encontrado que existen bajos niveles de magnesio en el suero y los tejidos de pacientes que sufren de migraña.

El magnesio es un mineral que comúnmente se encuentra en las dietas de las personas y que mantiene tonificados los vasos sanguíneos, reduce la excitabilidad de los nervios y promueve la relajación muscular.

La falta de magnesio en el organismo se asocia con síntomas como: cansancio, palpitaciones, debilidad muscular, espasmos y temblores, depresión, pérdida del apetito, dolor en los periodos menstruales, alta presión sanguínea y constipación.

Las personas que ingieren una alta cantidad de calcio, proteínas y alcohol, necesitan consumir más magnesio; mientras que la deficiencia de magnesio es más común en aquellas personas que toman potasio, laxantes o diuréticos.

Las personas que sufren de diabetes, enfermedades del riñón, hipotiroidismo y problemas de absorción de alimentos, también son más susceptibles a sufrir falta de magnesio.

Este mineral se puede encontrar en una variedad de fuentes alimenticias. La mejor de todas éstas son los vegetales frescos de hojas verdes. También se puede hallar en muchos tipos de nueces y alimentos basados en granos enteros, además de la soya. Los mariscos son otra excelente fuente que aporta magnesio al cuerpo.

Vitamina B2

La vitamina B2 puede aliviar los dolores de migraña. Los efectos máximos se podrían obtener después de tres meses de la ingesta diaria de 400 mg de esta vitamina.

La vitamina B2 tiene un gran potencial para ser usada en la prevención de migrañas. Las personas que tienen deficiencias de esta vitamina, a menudo presentan piel roja, grasosa y escamosa al lado de la nariz o en los genitales, labios pálidos y agrietados, picazón de ojos y excesiva sensibilidad a la luz.

Las dosis bajas de vitamina B2 se asocian con el consumo inadecuado de proteínas de origen animal y con el sufrimiento de diarreas crónicas, enfermedades del hígado, alcoholismo y uso, durante largo plazo, de anticonceptivos orales.

La vitamina B2 se encuentra en la leche, la carne y los huevos.

Herbolaria

De cierta manera, todos en algún momento de nuestras vidas hemos utilizado remedios naturales: el té de gordolobo para la garganta, el té de tila para los nervios y las hojas de lechuga para el insomnio que nos daban nuestras abuelitas. Éstos son remedios naturales que han sobrevivido gracias a la sabiduría popular y que, aunque lo parezcan, no son remedios mágicos sino curas basadas en la herbolaria.

La herbolaria es la ciencia que estudia las propiedades y poderes curativos de la gran diversidad de plantas y hierbas que nos provee la madre naturaleza. Tiene sus raíces en el origen mismo del hombre y en su necesidad de curar sus dolores, padecimientos o enfermedades.

Desde sus inicios, tanto las comunidades primitivas, como los egipcios, griegos y romanos, encontraron en la herbolaria el vehículo idóneo para cuidar su salud y tener una mejor calidad de vida, herencia que después se vio enriquecida de manera clave por la contribución del lejano Oriente y, sobre todo, por la vastísima tradición herbolaria del Nuevo Mundo.

El aprovechamiento de las propiedades curativas de las plantas es una práctica milenaria que nunca ha dejado de tener vigencia.

Todavía en el siglo XVIII, el tratamiento médico habitual en Occidente se basaba en la prescripción de remedios herbales y, actualmente, la Organización Mundial de la Salud estima que la herbolaria está tres o cuatro veces más difundida en el mundo que la medicina ortodoxa.

Más aún, se considera que casi la mitad de los medicamentos modernos proceden del reino vegetal.

La herbolaria no sólo se limita a recetar hierbas, sino que basa la curación en la dieta, el ejercicio y el equilibrio adecuado entre tiempos de actividad y de descanso, así como en la hidroterapia; es decir, el uso de baños y compresas frías y calientes como terapia.

La herbolaria nos invita a vivir en armonía con la naturaleza, consumiendo alimentos naturales y evitando la carne, el azúcar, los alimentos procesados, la nicotina y el alcohol para favorecer la salud y evitar la acumulación de toxinas en nuestro cuerpo.

La herbolaria busca deshacerse de las enfermedades, primero, dejando de añadir toxinas al cuerpo y, segundo, favoreciendo los procesos naturales de desintoxicación mediante el uso de hierbas y de hidroterapia.

La herbolaria ve al individuo como un ser complejo que funciona en los niveles físico, mental y espiritual. Nos enseña que es posible estar sanos cuando comprendemos que ciertos tipos de actitud y hábitos mejoran nuestra salud, mientras que otros son dañinos.

Los factores que tienen mayor influencia en nuestra salud son nuestras emociones y pensamientos, la alimentación, el descanso y el ejercicio.

Las actitudes y pensamientos negativos producen en nuestro organismo respuestas fisiológicas que, al final, producen estreñimiento, desequilibrios nutricionales, úlceras, hipertensión y otros problemas.

El miedo, el enojo, los celos, la preocupación, la vanidad, el odio, la envidia, entre otras, son actitudes negativas y destructivas para nuestro organismo; en cambio, las actitudes y los pensamientos positivos como la fe, la esperanza, la compasión, la valentía, el perdón y el amor son un fuerte potencial de curación para nuestro cuerpo.

Como en todas las terapias que hemos expuesto en este libro, la herbolaria requiere un esfuerzo; no basta con tomar algunas cápsulas herbales y beber algunas tazas de té amargo para lograr controlar la migraña. Es necesario comprometernos a mejorar nuestro estilo de vida mediante cambios en nuestra dieta, que incluyan un mayor consumo de frutas y verduras que ayuden a limpiar el cuerpo de las toxinas acumuladas, refuercen las funciones naturales y ayuden a los procesos de curación, así como eliminar el consumo de comidas chatarra, alimentos procesados, alcohol y tabaco que dejan un residuo de toxinas en nuestro organismo; todo esto para lograr una mejora real y a largo plazo.

Por otra parte, debemos darnos tiempo para hacer ejercicio, éste fortalece el corazón, los pulmones y la circulación, además de favorecer, la producción de endorfinas. El ejercicio regula el apetito y el peso corporal, ayuda a eliminar el estrés, el insomnio y mejora la concentración.

De la misma manera que requerimos actividad física, necesitamos del descanso. Buscar el tiempo para dejar de lado nuestras obligaciones y dedicarnos a disfrutar de la vida respirando aire fresco y contemplando la naturaleza, logra que renovemos nuestras fuerzas y nuestras motivaciones para seguir adelante.

Descansar durante periodos de trabajo intenso, impide que se presenten enfermedades que nos obligarían a dejar de lado nuestras actividades.

En resumen, la terapia naturópata nos invita a buscar una actitud positiva ante la vida, llevar una dieta adecuada y encontrar un equilibrio entre ejercicio y descanso, entre nuestras obligaciones y el tiempo de relajación; con esto, no sólo alcanzaremos la salud, sino que aprenderemos a apreciar lo maravillosa que es nuestra vida.

La herbolaria tiene varios métodos de aplicación; estos métodos se pueden dividir en dos categorías importantes: las aplicaciones internas y las externas. Una aplicación interna es todo lo que se ingiere y después se absorbe y transmite a través de la sangre o es asimilado directamente en el tracto gastrointestinal.

Las aplicaciones internas pueden presentarse como tabletas, cápsulas, tinturas, tes y jarabes.

Las aplicaciones externas son las que se utilizan para tener efecto en el área en que se están aplicando. Ejemplos de éstas son las compresas, los fomentos, los enemas, las gárgaras y los linimentos.

A continuación presentaremos los principales remedios naturistas, utilizados para tratar la migraña y su forma de aplicación.

Aguacate

(*Persea americana*)

Es un árbol que alcanza 20 metros de altura, de tronco grueso y con hojas alargadas que terminan en punta. Las flores son pequeñas y sus frutos son ovalados, con semilla grande rodeada por la pulpa carnosa.

Se cultiva por sus frutos y crece asociado con la selva tropical; crece en climas cálidos o templados y, para fines terapéuticos, se usa la cáscara de la semilla, la del fruto o las hojas. Las hojas se usan para curar el dolor de cabeza por migraña. Ponga a hervir un puñito de hojas por 10 minutos en un litro de agua y tome esta infusión tres veces al día mientras dure el dolor.

Alholva

(*Trigonella foenumgraecum*)

Prepare una infusión remojando las semillas de la alholva de cinco a 15 minutos.

Beba una taza al día, caliente o fría.

Albahaca

(*Ocimum basilicum*)

La albahaca es cultivada mundialmente como una planta anual. Muchas variedades tienen composiciones y sabores diferentes. El té de albahaca es muy bueno para combatir la migraña. Prepárelo poniendo a hervir una pizca de albahaca seca en medio litro de agua y tomando una taza de este té al día.

Las compresas de albahaca también son efectivas para tratar el dolor de cabeza por migraña. Ponga una cucharadita rasa de albahaca seca en polvo en una taza de agua caliente durante 10 minutos. Cuele el líquido. Cuando se enfríe, agregue dos cucharadas de hamamelis puesta a refrigerar previamente. Aplique la solución como una compresa sobre la frente y sienes.

Banana o plátano

(*Musa sapientum*)

El plátano o banana es una planta que crece hasta seis metros de altura. Se cultiva mundialmente en las regiones tropicales.

Para aliviar los dolores de migraña, haga una cataplasma de cáscara de banana madura y aplíquela en la frente y en la parte posterior del cuello durante el dolor de cabeza.

Calabaza pumpkin

(*Cucurbita pepo*)

La calabaza pumpkin es la tradicional del día de muertos. Es una variedad de la calabaza de invierno; su forma es redonda y de color anaranjado.

Para aliviar el dolor de cabeza por migraña, utilice la pulpa raspada de la calabaza *pumpkin*, o la calabaza amarilla o anaranjada, y aplíquela sobre la frente y las sienes como ungüento.

Dondiego de día

(*Ipomoea purpurea*)

Es una planta bastante común que crece con frecuencia como una hierba mala en los terrenos húmedos. Su tallo trepador, que se expande como enredadera, puede cubrir un área de hasta dos metros de circunferencia. Sus flores en forma de trompetas pueden tener diversas tonalidades, pero en su mayoría son blancas.

La tintura de flores de dondiego de día es útil para aliviar el dolor de cabeza por migraña.

Combine 1 1/2 taza de flores, finamente cortadas con una tijera, en dos tazas de ginebra. Póngalas en un frasco con una tapa ajustada y colóquelo en el marco de una ventana por dos semanas. Agite el contenido dos veces al día. Cuele a través de varias capas de gasa.

Empape un paño limpio con un poco de esta tintura, exprima el exceso y aplíquelo sobre la frente para obtener alivio.

Coloque una toalla pequeña sobre el paño, para evitar que el alcohol se evapore rápidamente.

Flor de la manita, mecapalxochitl o mano de león

(*Chiranthodendron pentadactylon*)

Es un árbol frondoso de 10 a 15 metros de altura, con hojas grandes cuyos bordes están terminados en punta. La flor es solitaria y de color rojo, muy parecida a una mano extendida, y los frutos tienen forma capsular. Habita en clima cálido, semicálido y templado. Crece como planta silvestre y se encuentra en el bosque mesófilo de montaña.

Se localiza, además, en Guerrero, Puebla, Estado de México, Centroamérica y Panamá.

El tratamiento más recomendado para tratar la migraña consiste en hervir la flor de este árbol con la de magnolia y de tila; la infusión se bebe por la mañana y por la noche.

Para calmar el estrés, se recomienda prepararla como té con hojas de magnolia, toronjil, hinojo, hierbabuena y flor de azahar; tómese como agua de uso.

Hierba Santa

(*Eriodictyon californisum*)

Para preparar un remedio para el dolor por migraña, haga una infusión, remojando durante 30 minutos entre 60 y

90 gramos de las hojas. Tómela tres veces al día cuando tenga el dolor.

Limón

(*Citrus limon*)

Los limones y las limas se desarrollan en plantas pequeñas, con espinas duras y afiladas. Son originarios de Asia.

Para aliviar el dolor producido por la migraña, se pone la cáscara de un limón pelado, con la parte blanca hacia abajo, sobre un pañuelo; se coloca sobre la frente, dejando la parte amarilla hacia la piel. Cuando sienta una sensación de ardor, retírela.

Otro remedio efectivo es respirar el vapor del agua caliente a la que se le haya vertido el jugo de varios limones; o dese baños de pies en agua caliente con limón, manteniéndose en posición vertical. El agua de limón caliente provoca una transferencia de la sangre de la cabeza hacia las manos, reduciendo la inflamación de los vasos sanguíneos de la cabeza.

Manzanilla

(*Matricaria chamomilla*)

La manzanilla es una hierba anual y fragante, con flores blancas que pueden alcanzar una altura de 40 centímetros. Las hojas son de color verde pálido. Se cultiva en Europa, Estados Unidos, Canadá y Argentina.

La manzanilla da excelentes resultados para tratar los dolores por migraña.

Prepare un té, poniendo en remojo, durante 40 minutos, dos cucharadas de flores frescas o secas de manza-nilla en medio litro de agua hirviendo. Cuele, endulce con miel y beba una o dos tazas al día por al menos 15 días.

Menta piperita

(*Mentha piperita*)

Es una hierba aromática perenne. Sus hojas son pecioladas. Crece aproximadamente un metro de altura y se cultiva en todo el mundo.

El té de menta piperita es excelente para el alivio del dolor producido por la migraña.

Ponga a hervir medio litro de agua. Retire del fuego, añada dos cucharadas de hojas de menta fresca o seca.

Tape y deje reposar durante 50 minutos; luego cuele. Beba de una a dos tazas de té frío cuando tenga el dolor de cabeza. Puede lograr alivio adicional frotándose un poco de aceite de menta piperita en las sienes y en la nuca.

Muicle, limalin, mohuite, muitle o mucle

(*Spicigera schechtendal*)

Planta que mide hasta dos metros de altura, con el tallo muy ramificado y hojas alargadas. Sus flores originan frutos con forma de cápsula. Habita en clima cálido, semicálido, seco y templado.

Crece cultivada en las casas y se asocia a la selva tropical y bosques de encino y pino.

Las partes que más se usan son las ramas, hojas y flores.

El cocimiento de éstas en infusión es un tratamiento muy útil para el dolor ocasionado por la migraña.

Romero

(*Rosarinus officinalis*)

Se emplean las hojas y las flores. Para tratar la migraña, prepare una infusión de romero remojando, de cinco a

15 minutos, 180 gramos de las hojas y flores de romero; tómelo durante los dolores de migraña tres veces al día.

Otra opción es preparar una infusión con partes iguales de romero y menta, y beber una taza caliente cada vez que se presente un dolor de migraña.

También puede aplicar un aceite de romero en la frente y sienes, el cual se prepara con una parte de romero por 10 partes de aceite vegetal.

Sandía

(*Citrullus vulgaris*)

Es una fruta grande, oblonga o redonda de una enredadera de la familia de los pepinos. Tiene una corteza dura de color verde (o blanca) y una pulpa roja con gran cantidad de jugo dulce.

Para aliviar el dolor de migraña, utilice la gruesa corteza de la sandía, atándola alrededor de la frente y sienes.

Sésamo o ajonjolí

(*Sesamum indicum*)

Es una planta anual con flores que tienen manchas blancas o pinceladas rojizas, amarillas o lilas. Las flores siempre se autofertilizan y producen sus semillas en cápsulas o vainas. Las semillas son diminutas, planas y ovaladas, con un extremo en punta. Contiene de 50 a 60% de aceite. Si se exprimen y se filtran, producen un aceite claro, amarillo pálido, sin sabor definido y comestible.

Para preparar un remedio para la migraña, ralle dos raíces de jengibre fresco hasta obtener una pulpa fina. Coloque dicha pulpa en dos capas de gasa y presione fuertemente para extraer de una a dos cucharaditas de jugo. Licue este jugo con tres cucharadas de aceite de semilla de ajonjolí y 1/2 cucharadita de jugo de limón.

Frote este aceite sobre la frente con un pedazo de tela de lino para aliviar la migraña.

Matricaria

(*Chrisanthemum parthenium L*)

La matricaria reduce la frecuencia de aparición de las crisis de migraña y atenúa los síntomas.

Prepare una infusión con una cucharada de matricaria por cada taza de agua. Deje hervir 10 minutos y tome tres tazas al día, antes de las comidas.

Acupuntura

La acupuntura es una ciencia, técnica o arte con una historia milenaria que data de ocho mil años a. C., por tanto, mucho más antigua que la medicina alópata, occidental u ortodoxa. Se ha practicado en los países orientales de forma tradicional por siempre, siendo expandida a Occidente en la segunda mitad del siglo XX, aunque se practicaba de forma esporádica por algunos médicos en países como Francia, Alemania, Rusia y Estados Unidos, entre otros.

La acupuntura se basa en la idea de que el cuerpo está recorrido por 12 meridianos que corresponden a cada función corporal. Cualquier anomalía en el flujo de la energía vital por estos canales, causa enfermedades que pueden curarse estimulando ciertos puntos situados a lo largo de cada meridiano.

Existen variantes de esta terapia dependiendo del instrumento u objeto que se use para estimular los puntos; éstas se definen de la siguiente manera:

Acupuntura: uso de agujas;

Digitopuntura o digitopresión: presión con los dedos;

Electropuntura: estimulación eléctrica;

Laserpuntura: estimulación con rayos láser;

Moxibustión: uso de calor.

El nombre de acupuntura deriva de las palabras latinas *Acus*, que significa aguja, y *Pungue*, que quiere decir penetrar. Técnicamente, la acupuntura se basa en la juiciosa colocación de agujas metálicas en determinados puntos del cuerpo humano. Consiste en la inserción de finas agujas de acero de hasta seis centímetros de longitud en los llamados puntos de acupuntura, haciéndolas girar suavemente entre los dedos pulgar e índice.

Este pinchazo preciso e indoloro en determinados puntos de la superficie del cuerpo estimula ciertos nervios, los cuales transmiten impulsos eléctricos a la médula espinal y los centros inferiores del cerebro y, desde allí, a la zona enferma.

La acupuntura es un tratamiento eficaz contra las migrañas. Así lo señalan investigaciones, las cuales revelan que las personas que sufren de migraña, y que han sido tratadas con agujas, sufrieron menos dolores de cabeza que los que recibieron terapias convencionales.

Este procedimiento eleva el nivel de endorfinas e incide positivamente en la serotonina, por lo que es efectiva contra varias formas de dolor, entre ellas la migraña; además, ayuda a controlar los estados emocionales, como el estrés, logrando así mejorar a las personas que sufren de migraña.

La acupuntura sólo debe ser realizada por un especialista, ya que las punciones deben ser más o menos profundas dependiendo de la dolencia a tratar.

Las enfermedades se asientan en la epidermis, la piel o el tejido subcutáneo; también en los vasos, los músculos, los huesos o la médula. Cada punción está destinada a alguno de estos niveles en particular, según el órgano a tratar.

El no realizar esta técnica de manera adecuada puede provocar un grave daño al organismo.

Además, la acupuntura está contraindicada en personas con alteraciones hematológicas o de las válvulas cardiacas, así como en las que toman anticoagulantes.

Auriculoterapia

La auriculoterapia es una rama de la medicina tradicional china que equilibra diversas funciones del organismo por medio de puntos de la oreja que, por un capricho de la naturaleza, están conectados a todos los órganos, vísceras y glándulas del cuerpo.

Utilizando esta técnica, que se basa en el principio de que no hay enfermedades sino desequilibrios energéticos en los seres humanos, el médico estimula los órganos en los que encuentra el desequilibrio, mediante un elemento de presión y estímulo que puede ser un balín de acero inoxidable, plata, oro o pequeñas semillas.

Se puede utilizar de forma temporal y/o permanente, con resultados muy significativos en enfermedades como hipertensión arterial, insomnio, estrés, ansiedad, dolores de dientes y migraña, entre otras.

La auriculoterapia reconoce en la oreja la imagen de un feto invertido, lo que significa que toda nuestra anatomía está representada en ella con más de 150 puntos de estimulación.

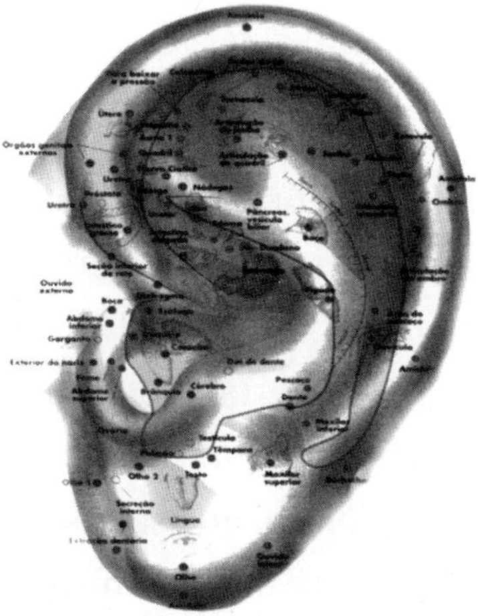

Cada punto de la oreja está íntimamente relacionado con los del cuerpo; por eso, la auriculoterapia puede combinarse con la acupuntura, electropuntura, digitopuntura (digitopresión) o laserpuntura.

El naturópata

Ante una enfermedad, el especialista debe estimular ciertos puntos en la oreja; al observar o palpar estos sitios, puede encontrar áreas dolorosas, más sensibles que otras, granos, zonas más cálidas o más frías, deformaciones, etc., lo anterior le ayudará a formar un diagnóstico y a determinar el tratamiento adecuado.

En el caso de la migraña, éstos son los puntos que se estimulan:

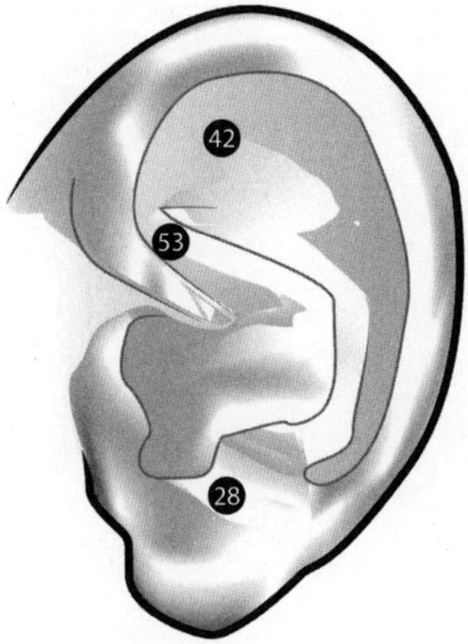

28 Sin mun de la oreja

53 Riñón

42 Subcorteza

La auriculoterapia es un sistema terapéutico y de diagnóstico que permite tratar un gran número de enfermedades como la obesidad, ansiedad, insomnio, adicciones, dolores óseos, digestivos, migraña, cefaleas, impotencia sexual y tabaquismo.

Aunque es una técnica sin riesgos, debemos destacar que no es aplicable a pacientes altamente debilitados y mujeres embarazadas con menos de cinco meses de gestación.

Migraña en niños

Muchos padres piensan que la migraña es algo que a los niños no les da, sino más bien algo que ellos nos provocan muy seguido.

Sin embargo, es un hecho que entre el 50 y el 70% de los niños en edad escolar ha padecido alguna vez de dolor de cabeza y, en cerca del 10% de los casos, se trata de migraña.

De hecho, la migraña es una causa constante de consulta médica en la edad pediátrica y, según estudios epidemiológicos, del tres al 11% de los niños menores de 15 años padece migraña, siendo el grupo de cinco a 13 años el que representa más del 90% de los casos, aunque se conoce de casos en los que este padecimiento se manifiesta desde los dos años de edad.

A diferencia de los adultos, la cantidad de niños y niñas que sufren de este padecimiento antes de la pubertad es similar; sin embargo, a partir de ésta, entra en juego el aspecto hormonal y entonces las mujeres son quienes sufren más de las cefaleas.

Las causas de la migraña en los niños son muy similares a las de los adultos, pueden deberse al entorno que los rodea: cambios de luz, sonidos intensos, cambios meteorológicos; además de cambios en sus hábitos de conducta: falta o exceso de sueño, omisión de una comida, cambios en la alimentación, etcétera.

En muchos de los casos, las migrañas en los niños comienzan cuando inician su etapa escolar, el adaptarse a nuevas rutinas, a sus maestros, a sus compañeros de clase, estar lejos de sus padres; es también en esta etapa cuando los pequeños comienzan a pasar más tiempo frente a computadoras, juegos de video y televisión y, por otra parte, es en esta edad cuando aumentan su consumo de comida chatarra: chocolates, refrescos de cola, pizzas, hot dogs, etcétera.

Al igual que en los adultos, es básico identificar cuál es la causa de la migraña y descartar que este dolor pueda ser el síntoma de un problema más grave. Es importante, si su hijo se queja de dolores de cabeza, que lo revise un oftalmólogo para descartar algún problema visual.

Además, existen dolores de cabeza potencialmente peligrosos que nada tienen que ver con una migraña, si es así, no dude en llevar a su hijo inmediatamente con un especialista:

- ✓ Si el dolor se encuentra acompañado de fiebre, vómito, entumecimiento del cuello, letargo o confusión.
- ✓ Si se presenta como una consecuencia de un golpe en la cabeza.
- ✓ Si ocurre por la mañana, acompañado por náuseas.
- ✓ Si aumenta en agudeza a lo largo del día o de un día para otro.
- ✓ Si sobreviene repentinamente después de un estornudo o tos.

Tome muy en serio el dolor de cabeza de su hijo y ayúdelo a describir su dolor ya que, en muchas ocasiones, el vocabulario limitado de un niño pequeño le dificultará describir lo que está sintiendo.

Por otro lado, a los niños les resulta más complicado que a los adultos manejar el dolor; ellos simplemente dirán que les duele y esperarán que alguien haga algo para solucionarlo.

Independientemente del diagnóstico que haga el pediatra y de las indicaciones que dé para el tratamiento, existen algunos remedios que le ayudarán a mitigar el dolor de su hijo.

Aplique compresas: algunos niños responden mejor a las compresas frías de agua y otros a las calientes, hágalo con la que a él le haga sentir más alivio. Mantenga la compresa por unos 30 minutos y vuelva a humedecerla cada vez que sea necesario.

Recuéstelo: el descanso es una de las mejores formas de alivio para un niño con migraña. No necesariamente tiene que dormir, con descansar unos 30 minutos será suficiente. Procure aislarlo del ruido y de la luz intensa, además de mantener alejados a los hermanitos ruidosos.

Masajes: un masaje relajante en el área del cuero cabelludo y las sienes podría ayudar al niño a relajarse si su migraña es causada por estrés. Sin embargo, en algunos casos puede resultar molesto, pues el cuero cabelludo puede estar muy sensible; de ser así, no insista y utilice algún otro método.

No lo mande a la escuela sin desayunar: Por ningún motivo permita que su niño se salte las comidas; además, póngale en su lonchera alguna colación sana para evitar que consuma comida chatarra en la escuela; aunque los niños pueden ser renuentes para comer verduras, pruebe con jícamas o zanahorias ralladas y jugos de frutas. Intente que su hijo evite las salchichas, los refrescos de cola, las pizzas, los chocolates y los cacahuates, tal vez estos alimentos sean los detonadores de las migrañas.

Déjelo divertirse: en algunas ocasiones, los niños en edad escolar se toman demasiado en serio sus responsabilidades, en la mayoría de los casos presionados por los padres quienes les exigen excelencia académica y se enfocan únicamente en el estudio, dejando de lado el juego. Si éste es el caso de su hijo, él y usted deben aprender a equilibrar el estudio y otro tipo de actividades más relajantes; si usted presiona a su hijo para que sea perfecto, quizá no sólo logre causarle dolores de cabeza, sino más adelante buscará también ser físicamente perfecto y tendrá problemas de anorexia o bulimia.

Ayúdelo a tener un sueño reparador: la falta de sueño puede ser el disparador de la migraña de su hijo. Si padece insomnio, ponga atención a la recámara de su hijo, fíjese que no sienta demasiado frío ni calor, que no haya mucho ruido, apague las luces pero deje la puerta medio abierta o ponga una pequeña luz nocturna si al niño le causa miedo la obscuridad; que duerma con ropa cómoda y que le permita transpirar, de preferencia pijamas de algodón; que no tenga en su recámara elementos que le distraigan el sueño como la televisión. Mándelo a dormir siempre a la misma hora y pídale que antes de dormir vaya al baño para que no se despierte por ese motivo. También puede ayudarlo dándole un baño de tina con unas gotas de esencia de lavanda o con hojas de lechuga una hora antes de dormir, o bien rociando en su almohada unas gotas de esencia de lavanda.

Enséñele al niño técnicas de relajación: estas técnicas son tan efectivas en los niños como en los adultos. Pídale que se imagine a sí mismo entrando en una tina de agua tibia, que trate de sentir cómo el agua va tocando sus pies, sus tobillos, sus rodillas, y así sucesivamente, que imagine cómo el agua va relajando su cuerpo. Trate de realizar este ejercicio junto con el pequeño para que él no se sienta presionado. Esta técnica requiere tiempo y paciencia de parte suya y del niño.

Alimentación: al igual que en los adultos, los desencadenantes de la migraña de sus hijos pueden ser ciertos alimentos.

En la dieta infantil, los alimentos que se han detectado como los principales detonantes de dolores de cabeza son, en este orden:

Leche de vaca
Huevos
Chocolate
Naranjas
Trigo
Queso
Jitomate
Carne de cerdo
Tocino, salchichas, jamón
Papas
Manzanas
Duraznos
Uvas
Plátanos, entre otros.

Procure eliminar estos alimentos de la dieta de su hijo por un mes e irlos introduciendo uno a uno, para detectar si alguno de ellos es el detonante del dolor.

Platique con su hijo: tómese el tiempo para conversar con él e investigar si hay algo que le está preocupando, si está demasiado presionado por los exámenes, si tiene problemas con sus hermanos o con sus compañeros de clases; hágale saber que lo que él siente es importante para usted.

Si después de observar los dolores de cabeza de su hijo no detecta algún factor emocional o relacionado con la dieta que los esté causando, ponga atención a su entorno, el clima, la humedad, etcétera.

Motívelo a hacer ejercicio: el ejercicio ayudará al niño a estar más relajado y le ayudará en la producción de endorfinas para atacar el dolor. En esta edad no se realiza entrenamiento de musculación (fuerza) con aparatos y/o pesas, sino que es preferible el entrenamiento mediante ejercicios dinámicos con el propio peso.

El organismo infantil está capacitado para soportar ejercicios de resistencia aeróbica. El desarrollo de las cualidades de coordinación motriz debe ser primordial. La velocidad es una habilidad de este tipo que en los niños mejora considerablemente si se trabaja de manera correcta.

Ejercicios prácticos:

1. Ejercicios para el desarrollo de fuerza:
   - ✓ Juegos de saltos con uno y dos pies (algunas rondas, avión, resorte, etcétera).

- ✓ Ejercicios de saltos utilizando bandas elásticas.
- ✓ Ejercicios de saltos con reata (individuales, parejas, etcétera).
- ✓ Ejercicios de saltos variados a lo largo de una escalera (tener el cuidado pertinente).
- ✓ Trepar y balancearse (pasamanos).
- ✓ Juegos con obstáculos.
- ✓ Ejercicios de lanzamientos con balones o pelotas, en diferentes formas (por arriba de la cabeza, laterales). No se recomienda usar pelotas con peso extra.

2. Ejercicios de flexibilidad:
    - ✓ Los ejercicios de estiramiento muscular no son muy recomendables en niños menores de siete años.
    - ✓ Para los niños menores de siete años, lo recomendado es permitir la movilidad natural de las articulaciones sin sobreesforzarlas.
    - ✓ Para los niños mayores de siete años pueden iniciarse algunos ejercicios de estiramiento,

pero con mucha atención en las articulaciones del hombro y la cadera, y en ningún caso es aceptado el sobreesforzar la articulación.

3. Ejercicios de resistencia:
   - ✓ Juegos de carreras a pie, en una distancia de tres km (carreras formando figuras).
   - ✓ Actividades en bicicleta.
   - ✓ Actividades en agua.
   - ✓ En este caso, la regla dice que los ejercicios deben exigir esfuerzos de larga duración y poca intensidad.

4. Ejercicios de velocidad:
   - ✓ Carreras de todo tipo (en forma individual o grupal).
   - ✓ Carreras de relevos.
   - ✓ Carreras de persecución.
   - ✓ Juegos (de búsqueda, con lanzamientos, con atrapadas, etcétera).

5. Ejercicios para coordinación:
   - ✓ Carreras de obstáculos para realizar en un tiempo determinado.
   - ✓ Lanzar y atrapar diferentes tipos de balones y objetos de forma variada (a distancias variadas).
   - ✓ Correr botando pelotas de diferentes tamaños, con uno o dos balones a la vez.
   - ✓ Nadar utilizando diferentes objetos en el desplazamiento.

6. Ejercicios para velocidad de reacción:
   - ✓ Reacción a señales acústicas diversas (silbato, palmada, grito, etc.) para iniciar un movimiento.
   - ✓ Reacción a señales ópticas como colores, desplazamiento de objetos, movimientos de otros compañeros, etcétera.
   - ✓ Movimientos de persecución (en tierra, agua, etcétera).

7. Ejercicios para el desarrollo de ritmo:
   - ✓ Ejercicios rítmicos en grupo (en gimnasia: marchando, corriendo, saltando, brincando; en natación: desplazándose, sumergiéndose, etcétera).
   - ✓ Ejercicios con balones, raquetas, bastones (individuales y en parejas).

8. Ejercicios para el desarrollo del equilibrio:
   a) Estático
      - ✓ Efectuar balanceos sosteniéndose en un solo pie.
      - ✓ Parado de cabeza con las manos.
      - ✓ Luchas en un área determinada.
      - ✓ Ejercicios con aros y balones.
      - ✓ Ejercicios sobre una viga de equilibrio a diferentes alturas.

   b) Dinámico
      - ✓ Ejercicios de atrapar objetos.
      - ✓ Ejercicios de brincar la cuerda con desplazamiento.
      - ✓ Circuitos de habilidad en bicicleta.

✓ Ejercicios en patines.
✓ Luchas con sacos.

Éstas son sólo algunas sugerencias de actividades que puede tener su hijo y que lo ayudarán a evitar los ataques de migraña, pero debe tener muy en cuenta sus gustos y preferencias y estimularlo a desarrollar actividades físicas que a él le gusten, para que no lo tome como una obligación sino como diversión.

Es muy importante que haga a su niño consciente de lo que le causa migraña; si se trata de algún alimento, no se limite a prohibirle que lo coma, explíquele que eso es el causante de sus dolores para que así deje de ingerirlo por su propia voluntad; asimismo, si la causa son demasiadas horas frente a la televisión o a los juegos de video, hágaselo entender hablando con él y no sólo le diga que es una orden de sus padres.

Más remedios

Casco de barro

Mezcle barro con té de árnica, dándole consistencia de masa, y aplique en cráneo, como si fuera casco de soldado.

Lo recomendable es dejarlo aplicado durante 30 minutos diarios, durante 20 días.

Baños de piernas

Prepare un recipiente con agua de árnica y una cucharadita de vinagre blanco (lo suficientemente alto para introducir las piernas). Hierva durante 10 minutos y agregue 10 cucharadas de barro, deje entibiar e introduzca las piernas durante 20 minutos diarios por 25 días.

Mascarilla de barro

Aplique en la cara con un espesor de dos centímetros durante 20 minutos diarios por 20 días.

Collarín de barro

Mezcle barro con té de manzanilla y árnica con tres gotas de vinagre; que tenga consistencia de masa de tortilla y con un espesor de tres centímetros. Aplique en cuello, como un collarín, durante 30 minutos cada tercer día, durante dos meses.

Chiquiadores de barro

Mezcle barro con té de árnica y ortiga; agregue dos gotas de vinagre y aplique una cataplasma del tamaño de una moneda, de unos cuatro centímetros de diámetro, en la sien, dando un masaje circular.

Colóquelo en ese lugar diariamente por 30 minutos duante un mes.

Acupresión

En el momento que sufra del dolor, es recomendable que presione la membrana entre el dedo pulgar y el índice de una mano, con los dedos pulgar e índice de la otra.

Cáscara de plátano

Coloque una cáscara de plátano en la cabeza.

Zumo

Prepare un zumo con dos ramas de apio y 300 gramos de col. Tómelo en ayunas.

Ceniza vegetal

Caliente un poco de agua y viértala en una palangana. Añada un puñado de ceniza vegetal y remueva un poco el agua.

Tome un baño de pies de entre 10 y 15 minutos.

Gasas

Coloque una gasa mojada en agua caliente sobre la frente hasta que se enfríe. Sustituya por otra gasa mojada en agua fría y déjela durante media hora.

Sábila, coñac y miel

Ingredientes:

Tres hojas grandes de sábila

Tres a cuatro cucharadas de coñac (aguardiente o tequila)

1/2 kg de miel pura de abeja.

Limpie las hojas, quíteles las espinas laterales y trócelas. Ponga el coñac (aguardiente o tequila), la miel y los trozos de sábila en la batidora. Una vez batido, pase el preparado a un recipiente de cristal.

Tome una cucharada 15 minutos antes de las comidas.

El estómago debe estar vacío o, al menos, deben haber transcurrido dos horas desde la última comida.

Baños de pies

Por muy curioso que parezca, un baño de pies puede curar el dolor de cabeza producido por la migraña, porque con él se favorece la circulación de la sangre. Además, al mismo tiempo, nos relajamos.

Ingredientes:

Una cucharadita de mostaza

Dos puñados de sal marina

Un vaso de agua.

Disuelva la sal y la mostaza en agua caliente. Tome el baño de pies por unos 30 minutos.

También se puede preparar un baño de pies hirviendo 1/4 de kilo de jengibre fresco en 1/4 de litro de agua. Después, diluya con la cantidad suficiente de agua para el baño de pies. Mantenga caliente el agua.

Mientras toma el baño de pies, puede beber un té de salvia, menta, valeriana o manzanilla.

Fomento de vinagre

Ingredientes:

Vinagre de vino o manzana

Esencia de manzanilla

Caliente ligeramente un poco de vinagre en baño María y viértalo en una taza. Para terminar, añada unas gotas de esencia de manzanilla y aplique con paños en el área de la frente.

Inhalaciones

Hierva dos litros de agua, apague la estufa y añada 15 gotas de aceite de eucalipto o menta en el agua. Cubra la cabeza e inhale los vapores de la olla.

Bálsamo del tigre

Frote este ungüento en la frente, de preferencia mientras toma baños de pies.

Esto alejará la sangre hacia la parte inferior del cuerpo.

Papas

Un remedio antiquísimo contra la migraña: pele y lave una papa, córtela en rebanadas y empápela en vinagre de manzana. Colóquela sobre una toalla o gasa húmeda, envuélvala y colóquela en la frente. Recuéstese en una habitación oscura y sin ruido.

Zumo de jengibre

Ingredientes:

Un trozo de jengibre (de un cm aproximadamente)

Tres hojitas de menta

Dos zanahorias

1/2 manzana.

Se licuan los ingredientes y se toma fresco.

Lavanda

Aplicar una gota de lavanda en cada orificio de la nariz (nota: la mayor parte de los aceites esenciales no deberían ser aplicados directamente, pero la lavanda es una excepción).

Inhale y relájese.

Menta y romero

Ingredientes:

Dos gotas de menta

Una gota de romero

Dos cucharadas de aceite de almendra

Agregue la menta y el romero junto al aceite. Aplique sobre los puntos dolorosos o sobre la nuca.

Comentario final

Ponga en práctica todos los consejos de esta guía y no se dé por vencido.

Utilice la alternativa que más le dé resultados, combine varias de estas terapias poniendo todo su empeño y dedicación y, si es necesario, no dude en acudir a un especialista.

Lo importante es saber que sí hay solución para los dolores de cabeza por migraña y que no tiene porqué resignarse a vivir con ellos.

Está comprobado que, eliminando los detonadores, el 80% de los dolores de migraña se puede evitar. Una vez que identifique cuáles son los factores que desencade-nan sus ataques migrañosos, siga esta guía:

Factores causantes	Qué puede hacer usted
Estrés (psíquico y físico). Los ataques de migraña suelen presentarse por la mañana.	Con un horario flexible se pueden reducir los ataques. Pruebe la homeopatía, aromaterapia, musicoterapia, herbolaria y/o masajes.
Sueño (demasiado o muy poco).	Intente dormir lo justo y regularmente. Pruebe la aromaterapia y/o herbolaria.
Comidas irregulares y ayuno.	Evite estar con hambre: coma a sus horas
Vino tinto y quesos fuertes.	Evite los alimentos que contienen tiramina. Revise la terapia alimenticia.

Factores causantes	Qué puede hacer usted
Algunos alimentos, como cítricos y chocolate.	Sea cuidadoso con dichos alimentos. Revise la terapia alimenticia.
Hipoglucemia,	Controle de vez en cuando el azúcar de la sangre.
Factores hormonales (menstruación, ovulación o pastillas anticonceptivas).	Consulte con su ginecólogo o médico familiar para asesorarse. Pruebe con aromaterapia, homeopatía y/o herbolaria.
Factores ambientales (calor, frío, luz, sonido, olor y cambios en la presión ambiental).	¡Haga algo si puede!

Factores causantes	Qué puede hacer usted
Migraña por tensión física.	Utilice los ejercicios de relajación o ponga en práctica la aromaterapia y/o masajes.
Esfuerzo físico.	No se esfuerce cuando tenga migraña.
Alergia.	Evite diferentes alergenos.
Consumo excesivo de fármacos.	Planee con su médico un programa de desintoxicación.

Y recuerde que el factor emocional juega un papel muy importante, tanto para detonar los ataques como para evitarlos o aliviarlos; ponga todo su empeño en vivir con actitud positiva.

En vez de lamentarse porque padece migraña o cualquier otra enfermedad, ocúpese en encontrar una solución a su problema.

No envidie a los demás, no juzgue, no dañe a las personas con sus acciones, trate siempre de encontrar las cualidades positivas en la gente con la que se relaciona en vez de buscar sus defectos.

Viva en armonía con la naturaleza y con la gente que lo rodea.

Recuerde que cada segundo que desperdiciamos en odiar, en juzgar y en criticar es un segundo valioso que le estamos robando a nuestra felicidad.

Bienvenidos a mi mundo naturista,
bienvenidos al mundo naturista del Dr. Abel Cruz.

La lengua de los sabios adornará la sabiduría,
mas la boca de los necios hablará sandeces.
Los ojos de Jehová están en todo lugar.
Mirando a los malos y a los buenos.
Proverbios, 15:2-4.

Con infinito amor a mis hermanos.

Dr. Abel Cruz

COLECCIÓN SALUD

7 semanas que cambiarán su vida
Acné
Anorexia
Antibióticos naturales
Afrodisiacos naturales
Artritis
Asma
Bulimia
Celulitis
Cocina naturista para niños
Coma y baje de peso
Cúrese a través de la sensualidad
Cúrese a través de los tés
Diabetes
Diabetes, guía práctica
Felices sueños
Gastritis y colitis
Herbolaria casera
Herbolaria mexicana
Juguitos para niños
Meditación y juventud
Migraña
El mundo vegetariano del Dr. Abel Cruz
Naturismo en padecimientos comunes
Naturismo para mujeres
Nervios, estrés e insomnio
¡No más migraña! / Un tratamiento naturista
El poder curativo de la manzana
El poder curativo de la miel
El poder curativo de la papaya
El poder curativo de la sensualidad
El poder curativo de la soya
El poder curativo de las semillas
El poder curativo de los cereales
El poder curativo de los cítricos
El poder curativo de los chiles
El poder curativo de los hongos
El poder curativo de los jugos
El poder curativo de los tés
El poder curativo del aguacate
El poder curativo del ajo
El poder curativo del gingsen
El poder curativo del nopal
Preguntas y respuestas sobre el sida
¿Qué es el cáncer?
Salud con jugos
Salud con jugos II
Salud con licuados
Salud con sábila
Síndrome premenstrual
Las várices

¡No más migraña! / Un tratamiento naturista
Tipografía: *Marcos González*
Negativos de portada: *Daniel Bañuelos*
Negativos de interiores: *Daniel Bañuelos*
Impresión de portada: *Editores Impresores Fernández S.A. de C. V.*
Esta edición se imprimió en junio de 2005,
en *Editores Impresores Fernández S.A. de C.V. Retorno 7-D Sur 20 No. 23 México, D.F. 08500*